# The Chilled Parent

Effective Parenting –
Peacefully and Powerfully
(The P&P Approach)

'The Chilled Parent', Copyright © 2007 by Rita Offen,
email: rita@chilledparent.com

Published by Ecademy Press
Contact:
Ecademy Press
6, Woodland Rise
Penryn, Cornwall, UK
TR10 8QD
info@ecademy-press.com

Printed on acid-free paper from managed forests. This book is printed on demand, so no copies will be remaindered or pulped.

First edition, 2007

Cover design and typesetting by Charlotte Mouncey

Printed and Bound by Lightning Source UK and USA

ISBN    1-905823-19-3

         978-1-905823-19-2

# ABOUT THE AUTHOR

Rita Offen is a married mum with three children, a boy aged 13, and two girls aged 10 and 7. She was born in England, but spent her first 6 years in Brisbane, Australia. She returned to England, and now lives on the South Coast.

From the age of 18, she worked in Secretarial/PA roles until she gave up work to have her first child. At the first opportunity she trained to be a learning support assistant and worked with children with severe learning disabilities, then with teenagers with moderate learning difficulties.

As well as having a keen interest in the study of psychology, Rita Offen is a Blackbelt in martial arts and a dedicated community volunteer working with the elderly.

Through her pursuit of personal development, she became aware and inspired by the work of Wayne Dyer and Anthony Robbins, and the principles they teach, and has, since learning these, endeavoured to use these principles in her own life.

What she has learnt and experienced along the way with her own family, her work in schools, and her personal development, has led her to write this book which she shares with you today.

# ACKNOWLEDGEMENTS

I would like to thank authors and public speakers Anthony Robbins, Dr Wayne Dyer and Mark Anastasi for being such inspirational leaders, for sharing their message with the world, and for the impact their teachings have had on my life.

I would like to acknowledge my martial arts instructor, Master Lowndes of Blackbelt Leaders in Worthing for teaching me the valuable principles of leadership and success, for being the ultimate role model, and for his continuing and unfailing energy and dedication he invests in me and in all his students.

I would also like to thank my husband Peter, whose continual pursuit of his self-development brought these inspirational people to my attention, and for his help and support, not only with this book, but throughout our relationship. He has been, and continues to be, truly influential in my life.

And not to forget the kindness and generosity of those who gave their time and invaluable help to me in writing this book, namely Alison Milner, the East Worthing Babysitting Group, and the Book Midwife, Mindy Gibbins-Klein.

And of course, my dear children, for their continual patience and understanding whilst I have been writing, for putting up with my moods, and for being great teachers.

# TABLE OF CONTENTS

# TABLE OF CONTENTS (CONTINUED)

# INTRODUCTION

Do you wish you had more time to be with your family?

Do you feel you're on the rollercoaster of life, with little opportunity to relax?

Have you noticed that when you hear the sounds of happy children playing, or when they say lovely, quirky things only kids say, that you don't notice them or don't take in and appreciate them?

Have you wondered if you're doing the right thing? You've had plenty of advice but you're still unsure? Or, despite all of your efforts to do your best with your kids, things just don't seem to be turning out how you wanted, they misbehave, or they don't turn out to be the people you had hoped they would be.

Well, you'll be glad to know that you're not alone, that many other families are experiencing the same, so I am sure you will enjoy some of the true stories you'll find throughout this book.

I wish to congratulate you for having an open mind, for taking the step to educate yourself about how you can improve your family life.

Most people don't take this step, and carry on unquestioningly. I know there are many families who know they are doing the right thing for them, leading the life they want, and that's great. Because you're reading this book now, I take it you're looking for an alternative, and I'm honoured to be able to share my ideas and experiences with you.

As you read it, you will have to ask yourself: "What makes sense to me? What is common sense? What actually produces the RESULTS I WANT?"

This book was written to show you what I believe the most fundamental key to parenting is, how we don't have to allow our modern life to take us over, and how parenting isn't complicated. It needs a simple and natural approach.

With all the messages and expectations from society, schools, and mother-in-law, it is easy to feel overwhelmed. We somehow expect to be perfect, and we are the same with our children. We expect them to be perfect too. The reality is, no-one's perfect, and never will be. Wouldn't it be a boring world if we were? There'd be no "saying it with flowers", there'd be no out-takes, no-one would learn anything new because, well, they don't need to – they're perfect!

Likewise, I myself don't profess to be perfect. I'm writing this book so that I can hopefully help you, show you you're not alone, give you a new perspective on parenting, and more than anything, help you take out some of the stress and strain, because I care that you are able to experience and take in as much of the pleasures of being a parent, because this is what we don't necessarily enjoy in today's society, with the pressures coming in on us.

I must confess that in my household, even with three lovely children, we just weren't enjoying parenthood at all! We allowed work to occupy our minds so that we weren't able to sincerely enjoy time with family, nor fully be with each other. When I say 'fully' I mean, giving our attention totally to each other. We worried about our children's development and abilities at school, we compared them to other children. We felt guilty if we thought we weren't giving them the ultimate party, as others were doing, or the latest electronic toys. We would wonder if we were doing the right thing, and would unwittingly put our own limiting beliefs upon our children, and were quick to judge them. We allowed our own emotions to control how we treated them. Together with my husband we realised what was eroding our 'family time' and that our priorities had drifted to outside influences, like work.

On 1st January 2006 our 9 year old daughter suffered meningitis, a serious, life-threatening disease. Suddenly we were faced with the possibility that she would no longer be with us. Miraculously after two weeks in hospital, some of this in a Paediatric Intensive Care Unit, she came through and is now fully recovered. I believe that many events happen to us for a reason, and the uncertainty at that time was agonising and made us face up to important issues relating to our relationship with her. It taught us how precious parenthood is, and the paramount importance of the family unit in shaping the memories and futures of our children. So let's not forget that the family is Number 1, and all that other 'stuff' that life brings along, like work and school, they're things we must do, but they're not to take us over to the detriment of our personal relationships.

What's important? To bring a child into the world, and to help shape the future of that child, his joy, his confidence, his vision, is probably the most responsible job there is. And the most rewarding! It's to be enjoyed. After all, a family is precious, and before we know it, we're looking back and realise our children have suddenly grown up!

I found that there are three factors affecting our family life:-

1. Us, as parents, our behaviour, and how we treat others.

2. Society and it's expectations of us as parents.

3. Time – lack of it!

In this book you won't find detailed strategies on how to get your kids to clean their room, or how to potty train them.

What it will do is get you thinking about:-

1. Your time and what your priorities are.

2. Your family relationships and how they affect your kids.

3. Society's subliminal messages that put pressure on parents and children, how you can identify them, and how you have a choice to follow them or not.

4. How your behaviour and language affects your kids.

5. The most important skills a child can learn and how you play a major part in teaching those skills.

6. How your eating habits affect your health.

7. A different approach to discipline.

It will help you, I hope, to change your focus and hilight that happiness, confidence and self-esteem are fundamental qualities of life, and the internal messages (messages we tell ourselves in our head) control our happiness, confidence and lifetime achievements. Telling ourself "I'm not good at ......" or "I can't ......" are blocks to us achieving our best. A parent who is aware of this can empower her child to develop a healthy attitude and to better deal with those many hurdles that come along throughout life.

And finally, I have included a section on health. I believe our health is fundamental to our daily life, and to our future, and especially for our kids. I see about me so many obese or near-obese kids. I walked into a café the other day and a mother was spoon feeding her baby, who looked about 8 months old, with chocolate gateau.

There's heaps of research and information telling us about our modern diets and the increasing health risks resulting, but the ultimate role of changing habits for better health in the future is down to parents to educate their children. Helping them to form good habits and look after themselves now will set them up for good health as adults. Ideally habits are best formed at a young age. I'm sure you will agree that it's harder to get out of a bad habit than it is to get into a good one!

> *"Here's to health. If you haven't got your health,*
> *you haven't got anything".*
>
> My Aunty Nelly
> Coventry, England

This book holds a simple yet unique approach to parenting. It will show you how to manage your relationship with your children, giving you, the parent, the confidence to know you can create a harmonious environment, happy children and a great future for them. This approach gets you looking at YOU, the parent. It's down to you – you're the adult – you shape your family relationships because you're the role model.

I really think it unwise to believe it is the responsibility of politicians, the media or anyone in power to guide us in our lives and health choices. They have their own agendas. We must take total control and responsibility for our family life choices ourselves.

Parenting is not a complex process which we may be led to believe in our modern society. Look at it this way. Children have been brought up all around the world through the ages in many varied environments and cultures. Picture the baby carried in a simple cloth on his mother's back high up in the Himalayan mountains – he may lead a simple way of life with his family, but the same key principles of family life and relationships apply to him as to your kids. His parents are number 1. He relies upon them as his role models, from whom he learns his habits, both emotional and physical. His relationship with them is key, just as it is in our complex modern society.

It's at this point I'd like to tell you why I did not write this book. I did not write this book because I believe it's the only way, the parent's 'Bible' to perfect parenting, the only answer in our cosmic universe. The reason I wrote this book is because it's the way that's worked, and is still working, for me and my family. As you read it, you may guess that at times I haven't been a 'chilled' parent, and still find it hard at times! As I'm making my last changes to this manuscript it's the school holidays, the kids are around as you can imagine, and it's hard not to say "get lost, can't you see I'm writing?"! I do, however, believe I have one answer that can help you to see that, whatever your worries have been, you're not alone, and really, you're probably doing OK. I just ask you to put my strategies to the test, implement some or all of them, and see the change for the better.

The fundamental message I want to get across is that I don't think there's an absolute right way to be a parent. We get loads of advice from everywhere about what we should and should not do, but really all children are different. We try to do our best and what we think is right, and things still go wrong.

For example, a parent once relayed this story to me about her experience with her son.

"My oldest son was not allowed any toy guns because we did not like the principle of them.  When he was 18 months old he bit his toast into the shape of a gun and shot me with it!!  To make it all worse, when he was 14 years old he was with some friends at a local park and one of them had a replica gun. The group of them had been mucking around with it and someone called the police.  No prizes for guessing who was holding it when the police arrived.  I received a telephone call to say my son had been arrested and was being held in a police cell!  I was angry with the owner of the gun who did not speak up and say that it was his gun and not my son's.  On retrospect maybe I should have allowed him to play with guns as a child - who knows!!"

By reading this book my hope is that you will regain peace and harmony in your family life, that you be released from some of the worries and pressures of parenting, and it is my sincerest desire that you, the reader, will in turn tell others about these principles for the ultimate family life.

# Chapter 1

## WHY YOU MUST PUT YOUR FAMILY FIRST - TODAY!

The family is the fundamental foundation of our lives. It is where we spend our most formative years, our childhood, where we learn the most important habits that we take into our adulthood, and eventually pass on to our own children. This is why as parents we must make it our priority to put our family first, and take responsibility for all aspects of our own and our children's lives. We know our family is our priority, but we find ourselves washed along with the tide of time, carrying with it work commitments, school commitments, and, all too often, we find we are not living the life that, deep down, we want for ourselves or our children.

In today's hectic society, our home must be our haven where we can go for peace and harmony, so that we can relax and gather our thoughts, and re-charge our batteries. It's not the place for shouting, arguing, impatience and disrespect – that seems to go on outside everywhere, in the streets and on the television!

I believe that the problems in society today are caused by the breakdown of the family unit, the erosion of parents' rights and state intervention in family matters, and of course, the gradual drip feeding of complete and utter mind-numbing, brainless, moral-less, clap-trap on our televisions!

This is not, I know, news to you. It's a topical subject that's been bandied about in the media recently. Our older generation will tell us it wasn't like this in their day, but others will say it was, and that they just have short memories touched by sentimentalism.

There's plenty of talk about the changes in our world and our lives, but how much action do we see? Our children are tomorrow's leaders and their parents are their significant influence, so it's time for parents to act, not chat.

# Chapter 2
## CURRENT CRISIS

**Stress and depression in adults**

In the UK in 2004/05 it was estimated that around half a million individuals believed that they were experiencing work-related stress at a level that was making them ill, and 6,800 new cases per year of work-related mental health problems was estimated. (UK Health and Safety Executive)

In the USA, job stress is estimated to cost American Industry $300 billion a year, 40% of job turnover is due to job stress, 60% to 80% of on-the-job accidents are stress-related, 75% to 90% of all visits to primary care physicians are for stress-related complaints or conditions and health care expenditures are nearly 50% greater for workers who report high stress levels.
(The American Institute of Stress).

**Family break-up**

In the UK more than 40% of marriages end in divorce. The number of divorces granted in England and Wales in 2004 was 153,399. More than half of these couples had at least one child aged under 16.

In the USA, current statistics predict that 43% of all marriages will end in divorce.

**Mental health and behavioural problems**

A survey published in 2000 showed that 10 per cent of children aged 5 to 15 had a mental health problem. The three most common groups of childhood mental health problems are emotional disorders (such as depression, anxiety and obsessions), hyperactivity (involving inattention and over-activity) and conduct disorders (involving awkward, troublesome, aggressive and antisocial behaviour). (The Stationery Office. 2000, Mental health of children and adolescents in Great Britain.)

**Prescription drugs**

In the UK the number of children being prescribed drugs for so-called behavioural disorders has soared. Prescriptions of Ritalin rose to 359,100 in 2004, a rise of 344,400 since 1995. It is almost entirely prescribed to children under the age of 16, and it has been estimated that one in 20 children suffers behavioural disorders such as attention-deficit hyperactivity disorder (ADHD), for which Ritalin is prescribed.

In the USA 46% of Americans use at least one prescription drug daily. The total number of prescriptions in U.S. in 2001 was 3.1 billion, and the cost of prescriptions in U.S. in 2014 is projected to be $414 billion. Between 1985 and 1999 prescriptions for central nervous system drugs to children increased by 327%. (Greg Critser, writer on the politics of medicine. Author of "Fat Land: How Americans Became the Fattest People in the World").

**Lack of respect for those around**

including teachers and parents –there has been an increasing erosion of values which has crippled personal responsibility. You can see examples everywhere - shouting and swearing in the street, teachers finding it increasingly difficult to impose their authority upon badly behaved pupils, parents who cannot control their children. Some things may be changing though, as I know new legislation is underway to give teachers more powers to deal with disruptive behaviour.

**Childhood obesity and illnesses**

In the UK the number of obese children has almost doubled in ten years. This is serious news because obesity in adolescence is associated with the premature onset of Type 2 diabetes and cardiovascular diseases. It also increases the cancer risk by 21 per cent for girls and 14 per cent for boys.

In the USA more than 12 million children were identified as being overweight in the most recent survey conducted by the National Center for Health Statistics.

# Chapter 3

## EXPLANATION OF CURRENT CRISIS

**Time is scarce - Everyone is busy**

It seems a generally accepted fact. We are busy whatever age we are, young or old. Even young children at pre-school are busy. A day spent observing a pre-school would reveal that they are never still, never a moment exists when they are not kept occupied with something. All activities are planned carefully. It's a very structured environment. The same can be said at all stages of school. Any possible moment of 'void' will be filled. Whether your child is the first to change after sports, the first to finish their lunch, this moment will be filled with some sort of activity, whether it be watching a video, getting a book or game or finishing some work. This, of course, is indispensable for the teacher who has a large number of children who she or he must control. You may recall the saying 'The devil finds work (or mischief) for idle hands to do'.

A gentleman I met who regularly attends a retreat for meditation told me an interesting story about a local primary school that had unfortunately burnt down and whilst their temporary classrooms were being built the children used rooms at the meditation retreat for their lessons. When their stay at the retreat was over the children and teachers were asked to write their comments about their time there. Various points were mentioned, like the comfy chairs were good, but the most popular point made by both pupils and teachers was the time set aside each day for complete silence and relaxation – this was a practice that was built into the normal routine of the meditation centre. Both parties felt this was very beneficial and enjoyed it! Silence and relaxation – even kids need it!

**Busy Minds**

Our minds are occupied. The media - television, radio, and newspapers continually bombard us with information, news, current affairs and advertising. We may not always be aware of it, but the media generates fear in its recipients, fear of what's going on around us through crime and wars, fear of what might happen to us, and fear that we are powerless to protect ourselves. Media tells us that there is always something going on that we must know about, and there's always something we must have – huge breasts, skinny legs, luxurious homes – and we'll be able to have them if we play the lottery, or phone in on some premium-rate phone number and answer a ludicrously easy question to which the whole nation knows the answer! Odds are we've more chance of winning the lottery.

**Holidays**

There is a growing trend for us to choose busy holidays. Holidays where there are crowds of people, where numerous trips are organised, and where our kids can be looked after for us in Kids Clubs, where they can fill every waking moment with an activity. We stress ourselves out queuing to get on planes, and exhaust ourselves travelling in our pursuit of 'nirvana', and some way of escapism.

**Priorities wrong**

Work and school commitments take over our lives. Because we have deadlines to work to, and our time is not our own, work and school take first priority. We seem to be on a constant treadmill so we neglect basic principles, like a family meal together, family conversation, time for each other.

I realise that we need to have an education, an income or occupation, and we must also consider what is best for us and our family at the same time. My point here is to be aware of our priorities, and consciously balance them as best we can.

## Poor diet

Our modern life-styles mean that too often we buy ready-made meals. So much food sold in supermarkets is now so full of salt, sugar, additives, colourings and flavourings that for many of us our diet rarely consists of fresh, natural foods. The popularity of TV and computers means that we are less active too.

When we are ill we seek out prescription drugs for the quickest way to treat the symptom, rather than looking at the root cause of our illness.

So, in summary, we're not taking care of ourselves. Society has made us slaves to our work, school, the media and consumerism. The basic and most crucial foundation for a healthy life has been eroded – the family – through the erosion of our time for one another and the distraction of everyday life.

Financial pressures are so often the cause of relationship break-downs. We are a consumer society and so much more today, people take out loans and buy new cars rather than buy an old banger. They spend their hard-earned savings on dream holidays rather than use the money to ease the pressure from other financial commitments. I'm not sure whether the TV ads have a large part to play in influencing us, but it is said that TV ads _do_ work, or they wouldn't still be making them! The need to have these luxuries today puts pressure upon us financially, and ultimately puts pressure on our relationships.

So, could you call this an alternative approach?  Yes, in the sense that, having witnessed the spiralling of society away from the principles of nature (peace, sanity and simplicity), to modern life (noise, chaos) and a tendency for us to need to 'escape', to find something else.  The TV programmes offering the idea of moving abroad to the sun, or buying our ideal home, or 'having all we want', are there to feed our need for 'escapism'.  I believe we have it all <u>here</u>, <u>now</u>.  We're just not tapping into it, because we're being told that in order to be happier, better, more attractive people, we need this, we must have that, be it a facelift, a new life, or garden decking!

Some of the ideas in this book may be difficult to follow at first, but I know that if I'd had this information five years ago it would have been much easier!  But it's OK!  If you missed the lesson first time around, how can you put it right?  Make a new start.  Old habits may have got you into trouble now, but this may be one way to put it right.

# Chapter 4

## WHAT CAN WE DO?

## TAKE CONTROL AND RESPONSIBILITY FOR YOUR OWN LIFE

<u>Decide now to stop and think.</u>  How is your life right now?  What are your family relationships like?  Where are your priorities?  For example,  one day I came to the realisation that I rarely spoke to my son.  All of a sudden, it seemed, he was 11 years old.  Between birth and 11 years we had, of course, spoken, but not really spoken nor been really close.  We hadn't had meaningful time together.   Little had I noticed that I could have given so much more.  For example when I was cleaning the house and he asked me to play, I could have stopped what I was doing and given him my attention, even if it was just for a bit.  I realised that, before long he'd be grown up and left home, and I'd be wishing I'd stopped, put the mop down, and done the proper thing, made a difference to his life, given him a bit of my time, showing it mattered.

<u>Do you have clear principles on which you live your life or are you confused?  Do you allow others to influence your life?</u>  The media are continually telling us what we want – have this, buy that, you're healthier if you buy this, you're sexy if you buy that.  Is it no wonder we feel we are not in control and directing our lives the way we want to go?

<u>Do you allow outside influences to affect how you feel?</u>

If we are dependent on other people and outside circumstances, we lose our own power, and we give power to others.  For example, if things are going well at work or school, we feel good, if things go bad, we feel bad, and we are on a constant rollercoaster of emotions.  It's

OK when things are going great, but we need to be able to master the times when things are not going the way we want, and not allow circumstance or people to influence our behaviour. I know this is hard, but I've regretted not enjoying an outing with my family or being able to take in the joys around me because I'm thinking about something that's not going so well for me. I suppose what I'm saying is that we parents need to look inside ourselves and get ourselves right so we can manage our emotions to deal with all the challenges of parenting, and be able to guide and empower our children.

# Chapter 5

## WHAT SIGNALS ARE YOU GIVING OUT TO YOUR KIDS? PATIENCE AND LOVE, OR FRUSTRATION AND AGGRESSION?

How often do we shout at our kids because we have something on our mind, or something niggling us?　We're following a train of thought, only to be interrupted by "Mum, can I have a plaster, I hurt myself".　After you've inspected it with the magnifying glass, they insist they must have a plaster, it hurts.　And all you want to do is to get on with your next task.　It takes the patience of a saint to keep our frustrations in, patience which we might not have an unending supply of, and we tell them to go away, or we vent our anger in some way.　Isn't it true we treat our family members differently to people outside the family home?　Even strangers get the best treatment.

## F A M I L Y

### By Author Unknown

*I ran into a stranger as he passed by,*

*"Oh excuse me please" was my reply.*

*He said, "Please excuse me too;*

*I wasn't watching for you."*

*We were very polite, this stranger and I.*

*We went on our way and we said good-bye.*

*But at home a different story is told,*

*How we treat our loved ones, young and old.*

*Later that day, cooking the evening meal,*

*My son stood beside me very still.*

*When I turned, I nearly knocked him down.*

*"Move out of the way," I said with a frown.*

*He walked away, his little heart broken.*

*I didn't realize how harshly I'd spoken.*

*While I lay awake in bed,*

*God's still small voice came to me and said,*

*"While dealing with a stranger, common courtesy you use,*

*but the children you love, you seem to abuse.*

*Go and look on the kitchen floor,*

*You'll find some flowers there by the door.*

*Those are the flowers he brought for you.*

*He picked them himself: pink, yellow and blue.*

*He stood very quietly not to spoil the surprise,*

*you never saw the tears that filled his little eyes."*

*By this time, I felt very small,*

*And now my tears began to fall.*

*I quietly went and knelt by his bed;*

*"Wake up, little one, wake up," I said.*

*"Are these the flowers you picked for me?"*

*He smiled, "I found 'em, out by the tree.*

*I picked 'em because they're pretty like you.*

*I knew you'd like 'em, especially the blue."*

*I said, "Son, I'm very sorry for the way I acted today;*

*I shouldn't have yelled at you that way."*

*He said, "Oh, Mom, that's okay.*

*I love you anyway."*

*I said, "Son, I love you too,*

*and I do like the flowers, especially the blue."*

Some might say relationships are a complex subject. We're all different, we deal with our kids differently, either because of their gender, personality, abilities, or their position in the family. We try to treat them all the same but it doesn't work that way.

All this may be so, but there are basic rules of human behaviour we can follow that are so simple, yet <u>powerful</u>, and will form a good relationship with our kids. Not only this, but will create a good environment in our home – a happy and peaceful environment.

# Chapter 6

## THE 7 RULES OF HUMAN BEHAVIOUR THAT ARE KEY TO A GOOD RELATIONSHIP WITH OUR KIDS

**1.      Keep your emotions under control**

What's controlling you?  Your mind or your emotions?  Is anger getting in the way of your rational thought?  OK, you say, how am I supposed to remain calm when my child has, despite being warned not to, wet my washing with the hosepipe?  Before you turn 'beetroot' red and shout "why did you do that?  I told you not to", stop and remember, kids don't think.  They're so wrapped up in their fun world, and they're not going to be able to tell you "why" anyway! They just did!  How about this instead - stay calm, point out what they've done, that next time what could they do to avoid it, or even, suggest a different water game with buckets and boats, or even, seeing as we parents tend to know what our kids are going to do before they do it, prevent the situation happening in the first place.

<u>If you can keep your emotions under control, your kids will respect you</u>.  Shouting and ranting doesn't gain respect.  I'd like to share an example here.  When my husband and I were in the early stage of our relationship, he went away for a week abroad on a training seminar.  This meant ultimately that I'd have to drive his fairly new car and pick him up from the airport on his return.  His car was quite big compared to my old mini which I was used to driving, so I was understandably a bit nervous as I approached the airport multi-storey car park.  The car park was nearly full and there was a car close behind me, so I was forced, in my panic, to park in a tight space  (or so it seemed to me) next to a concrete pillar.  I completely ballsed it

up and the car ended up parked very crooked and lodged against the pillar! My quick-thinking told me it would be best not to try to move the car and make the dent and paint damage any worse. To anyone who saw it, it it would have made great conversation over the dinner table that night, because it was so laughable. I can imagine them saying "You'll never guess what I saw today. How could someone manage to do that?". I left the car parked like that and fortunately my embarrassment faded a little as I distanced myself from it, and made my way to the arrivals gate. As I waited, you can imagine what was going through my mind. Half an hour ago I couldn't wait to see him, but now I was dreading it – what will he say? He'll go mad! The air will be blue! He eventually appeared and smiled at me, so pleased to see me. Behind my false smile I thought "He's not gonna be smiling when I've told him what I've done!". Anyhow, I decided to get it over with, and told him straight away. When we got to the car he said nothing at first, remained calm, then suggested we don't start the engine but gently push the car out, with him negotiating the steering wheel, which we did. Of course, I apologised all the way home. But here's my point - he didn't shout, rant, criticise, he just said "don't worry, it was an accident". This was completely new behaviour to me. I realised that throughout my life, especially as a child, patience and understanding when it came to mistakes, were not common-place. I respected him for his reaction, and I believe that, in my mind, it sealed our relationship. The example he set taught me a lot about myself, how I perceive events and how I react.

And so this can be for our kids. I suppose I'm saying 'lighten up'. Put things into perspective. I've found that getting cross doesn't necessarily get the message across.

## 2.    Listen to the way you're talking to your kids

I once had a dear friend who, when she conversed with her son, would speak in a high-pitched tone, and moreover, it seemed to be a tone reserved only for him. When she spoke to other people the tone lowered and she spoke slowly and calmly. When she spoke to her son there would be an urgency to her message and a question or condemnation – "well, if you'd done what I said, this wouldn't have happened". Needless to say, the two of them didn't get on. He repeatedly caused trouble and rebelled, to his mum's dismay. I believe she just did not realise what she was doing, she couldn't hear herself speaking.

Kids pick up our tone, the speed at which we speak, the words we use, and they interpret them how they can. To keep our speech in a respectful manner towards our children, to be mindful of what we say and how we say it, can make such a difference to our relationship with them. Often we don't mean to speak in a certain manner, but we've been conditioned to speak that way, or we just don't think because we're occupied with other things at the time.

I comprehend myself that because it can be difficult understanding their behaviour sometimes, it shows in our voice, and there are times when it's necessary to get a point across. I'm sure you'll agree that children are often quite different when it comes to doing what dad says as opposed to doing what mum says. I've found it amazing how, when dad speaks, they just get on with it, but when I speak, they don't. Speaking to various mums, it seems I'm not alone. I think it's often the familiarity children feel about mum that makes them more likely to push the boundaries of behaviour and, maybe, not jump to her word. Because dad is the character who may only appear at evenings and weekends, they're a touch unfamiliar with him, might be less willing to test the boundaries, so do what he says. However, I must say, I've met a few mums who say dad's the one with whom the kids know they can get away with anything! I am aware, however, that because I have been known to give in to their demands to easily on past occasions, not stick to my word, and not enforce my own rules, my children won't do what I say the next time around.

I know too that I can just, in an impatient manner, dismiss what my child says, as though it's trivial to me, forgetting that, to him, it's probably not trivial, but really important. And I do this usually in an absent moment, when I'm busy, or from the mindset of "what you've got to say isn't important".

From time to time we need to remember to take their words as we would a respected friend's, to listen and respond with care and attention, even when busy. After all, isn't it true that we will usually find time even at the busiest moments for things that really matter to us?

## 3.      Love unconditionally

Whatever your kids do, right or wrong, they must know that you love them anyway. One way to illustrate this is by looking at the area of mistakes (theirs and ours). We all make mistakes, we have to, because mistakes show us what we need to improve and what <u>not</u> to do. Mistakes are the best way we learn, yet we often avoid situations in which we might make mistakes. If our kids are learning, growing, and trying new things, we can expect them to make mistakes, and lots of them. They don't enjoy it, but they're usually doing their best with what they know.

How you deal with this is crucial to how kids view their mistakes.

You can either:-

(i) React with "how could you have done that", "what's the matter with you?" or

(ii) Accept that they're doing their best. Look back to your own childhood. Did you do silly things that as an adult you're still ashamed or embarrassed about?

Kids who fear punishment or loss of love from their parents when they make a mistake learn to <u>hide</u> their mistakes. They learn to feel unworthy, and then aim to avoid mistakes in a quest to be perfect.

Love them unconditionally, accept their mistakes as the path to learning and growing, and help them to accept their mistakes freely and for them to ask rather "how can I learn from this?"

What I've learnt is, as best I can, not to react hastily or impatiently.

"One morning, whilst my husband and I were trying to have a well-deserved lie-in, our two year old daughter came into the room to tell us very proudly, in her squeaky excitable voice, "we've been having fireworks!". She looked so pleased with herself, grinning from ear to ear, but her five year old brother was hastily nudging her and looking a bit sheepish. Knowing what he's like (always up to what he shouldn't) we leapt out of bed to see what it was all about. In the dining room, under the dining table, we discovered a mass of melted plastic which, it turns out was the result of a lit candle with plastic shopping bags fed on top, in order to create a bonfire. It was completely melted into the carpet, the carpet ruined, fit only for ripping out. What did we do? Well, for a start, the look on our son's face told us he didn't need telling how serious this was. Secondly, it was so unbelievable, it was almost laughable, and thirdly, it was his sister's complete innocence when announcing it coupled with his dare-devil cheekiness that had us laughing. The carpet was so old and horrible anyway, it needed replacing. In fact, the room looked better with the carpet removed, so we saw an advantage from it. We did not get mad, but, of course, explained to them both the seriousness of playing with fire – how people can be easily maimed or killed, and that <u>never</u> to do it again. We carried on our day with nothing more said about it and no hard feelings. We did not allow it to affect our relationship".

I think this is a good way to be, not to hold on to anger or unbelief, to let it go, and carry on loving as normal.

*"Experience is the name everyone gives to their mistakes"*
Oscar Wilde

## 4.     Admit your own mistakes

The other day I was working at the computer and my youngest girl, who's a real talker, always buzzing with excitement about every-thing, persistently interrupted me to ask questions and to tell me things. My patience at its last drop, I turned around and shouted at her in my real 'I can't believe you' tone, "just go away and let me get on". She got the message and I know she felt hurt because she went away and did not come back. When I'd finished my work I had calmed down, and later on she was with me, talking and behaving as if nothing had happened (children are so forgiving. An adult would probably be giving me the silent treatment by now!), so I said "I'm really sorry I shouted at you earlier. I was getting uptight about my work, and I shouldn't have done that". She hugged me so tight and looked so happy. I could tell my words meant a lot to her.

If you do make a mistake, often the best way to deal with it is to admit you're wrong and apologise. Kids love it when their parents are wrong. It shows you're human, and that anyone can make mistakes. Apologising also shows you are aware of, you live, and you're willing, to stick by your own rules, and you'll gain much more respect this way from your kids. It will help to bond your relationship even more.

## 5.    Tell your kids you love them

Obvious I know, but how little or, at all, do we do this? I tell you, when you do, they love it. When I started doing this with my kids (and, yes, I wasn't even thinking of it before, I took it for granted that they knew I loved them), it turned our relationship around. It brought us so much closer, and guess what, those three little words started coming back to me.

A friend of mine told me a funny story about her girls when she was talking with them about loving each other:-

"My little girl Charlotte (age 4) said "I love Mummy, I love Daddy and I love Sophie" and so Sophie (age 2) copied her and said "I love Mummy, I love Daddy, I love Charlotte and I love Sophie". Charlotte giggled saying "Sophie said she loved herself!", then she went quiet, obviously thinking about this and said "Actually I love myself too". She had realised that although she initially thought her little sister was being silly, that it was probably a good thing to say you love yourself!"

Isn't it true that we do take this word 'love' for granted in our relationships, not just with our kids, but with partners, parents and family. For some, it's because it's not very manly to say it, and for others, we just feel uncomfortable. Maybe the discomfort comes from the fact that not many people are saying it – to say 'I love you' is out of the ordinary. But aren't these moments really special when someone does say it? It means so much to the receiver. I don't think it is said enough.

I met a man at a seminar once, who, in front of all the participants there, shared a story about his life. It was about his relationship with his father. He spoke such harsh words about him, and he described their relationship as being 'cold'. It seemed to be that he felt they had not had a close relationship throughout his life. His dad went about his life, and the son felt his dad did not care about him because they rarely talked or shared anything. The son went through his life literally believing his dad to be a cold, unloving man when really, deep down, he wasn't. He had made these stories up in his head based on what he believed was happening, having not spoken a word to find out the truth.

He'd held onto these feelings to this day until recently he spoke his feelings to his dad, he let go of those hard feelings and said what he'd always been feeling deep inside … "I love you", and that moment completely turned their relationship around, a relationship they both cherish and enjoy today. He discovered through talking with his dad, of course, that his dad had always loved him, but had never expressed it to him, although had <u>wanted</u> to express it to him, just didn't know how to, and was now so grateful to have the opportunity opened to him to express it now.

What I'm saying is, don't leave it unspoken or rarely spoken until your kids are 40 years old, but do it now. Our behaviour does not necessarily speak about the real person we are. We may not act as though we love or feel for a person, but inside we do, and sometimes it's necessary to make this clear to them.

### 6.     Take time to talk to your kids

Spend time with your children to talk to them in quiet surroundings, away from interruptions, and if you have more than one child, make sure you do this for each of them, one to one. This way you can have a really good conversation about their day, or about anything.  I have what I call 'cuddle time' with my girls in the evening when I can, and I know it's important to them.  The best thing about it is, because I'm willing to share a little of my time to be with them alone, we have interesting, precious conversations that just wouldn't happen in the company of others who would be butting in or competing for attention.  And they're also willing to share information about things they may not want to share in front of their siblings.  These are priceless moments, especially with teenagers, who are feeling a little self-conscious, don't want to appear weak, or to show their personal concerns in front of others.  It's when you are alone they are more likely to open up and you can help them how you like, but don't be surprised, of course, being teenagers, when they don't take up your suggestions! 'They know best'!

"I was finding that in the evening, when dinner was cleared, baths were done and it was time to relax with my two girls, we were frequently interrupted by telephones ringing, either the home or mobile phone.  One day I made myself a new rule – not to answer the phones during this time.  I could check later who had called, and then return their call later.  This made such a difference with no more interruption or frustration.  I chose this time to be for <u>us</u>."

## 7. Listen to your kids

This is how you build trust and openness, strengthen your relationship and create closeness. Humans need to be understood. If you're not listening to your child, he knows! By listening you're showing him that what he has to say is important, and that you're making the effort to understand him.

I found I wasn't listening. I did, and still do, make the common mistake of assuming I know what they are going to say, and butting in before they've finished. Test this out yourself with your family and with friends. It's surprising how often we do not listen. Children notice this too. They may not consciously identify that we are not listening to them, but they are subconsciously aware of it, and they themselves make the same mistake of not listening. Parents can help them to become better listeners by pointing this out, and by setting the example and being good listeners themselves.

I'm sure you're thinking it's not easy to be a good listener all the time. It's true, it's hard to be doing two, three, four things at once <u>and</u> listen to your kids at the same time. A great example came up the other day when I was rushing around as usual, and I asked my daughter if she got to sleep OK that night. Her reply was "Yes, it only took me three hours to go to sleep" (she's a professor of sarcasm), to which I replied ""Oh good, that's OK then". Moments later, I was faintly aware of her sniggering away with her sister, because they had seen the insaneness of my response and they knew 'mum's not listening again, she's doing her pretending to listen thing'.

The ability to listen and to 'be' in another person's world is a magic component of forming good relationships. People love it when you listen to them. When I mean 'listen', I mean shutting out the noise from around you, taking in the words they say, and allowing them the time and space to express themselves before responding. People love to talk about themselves and to feel that what they have to say is important to others, because what they have to say is important to them. For children, it matters more than anything that who they are and what they have to say matters to their parents.

The last two points above are so simple, yet so powerful. It just needs a little of your time. It doesn't even have to be much time.

These simple rules are relevant to whatever age your kids are, and in applying them you will build on to your relationships or mend them, whatever your needs. I found that when my son reached 12 years old he would 'disappear' into his own world, speak more to his friends and very little to me. He had a whole life going on that I didn't know about. By taking a little time out whenever convenient to talk, we keep communication going. I'm not saying I fire questions to find out what he's been up to! Sometimes I don't think I want to know! But I give him the freedom to talk about whatever he wants, if he wants to. It would be so easy not to, but at times like this it is down to us parents to make the effort, or it might not happen.

# Chapter 7

## ARE YOU EMPOWERING OR DIS-EMPOWERING YOUR KIDS?

Personal power is the self-belief and confidence to know that you are capable of anything you set your mind to. It means you feel good about yourself and that you do not rely upon others' opinions to feel good about yourself.

Children are born with an amazing amount of confidence. They believe they can do anything, and won't give up until they do or get what they want. If we had their confidence and beliefs, what amazing things could we achieve as adults - we could accomplish our dreams!

> *"Maybe" means "Yes"*
>
> Charlotte, age 6

Unfortunately through life children pick up enough messages to the contrary. Of course, it is necessary to guide children sometimes for their own safety, where there may be danger, and also to make them aware of what is right and wrong, but there are ways of teaching children that empower them to feel the confidence to try new things and focus on their abilities rather than their failures:-

**Look for the best in your kids**

Don't we have a tendency to see what's wrong with something rather than what's right? As I said before, kids are doing the best with the resources that they have, so whatever happens, for example, they come last in the sprint race at Sports Day, they forget to put the raising agent in the cake, or they break all the eggs carrying them home from the shops, look for what they've done well. I bet they'd tried hard in the race, baked the cake with care and enthusiasm, did their best to help by getting the eggs. Praise them for what they've done well, look for what they do right rather than what they do wrong.

This is not something that comes naturally to some of us, especially me. On one rare occasion when my girls tidied their bedroom (I think it was because a friend was coming to stay for a sleepover and they needed to make space for the camp bed). There was a lot of shuffling around upstairs, and slamming of cupboard doors. They were putting everything away, hanging clothes up, putting a month's-worth of dirty undies in the wash basket, returning Barbie's items to her box. Proudly they called on me to perform the inspection. Still puffing from the exertion (no, not me climbing the stairs – them from working), looking proud, they awaited my verdict. It looked great. Clearly they'd made a big effort. However, for some reason, my eyes couldn't avoid the way the board games had been stuffed under the bed in a haphazard manner. My natural tendency came over me. I took a breath as though to say "that's great, but ...... the games are messy", and fortunately stopped myself and changed it, to their delight, to "that's fantastic, it looks great".

I thought the praise might encourage them to tidy their room more often but, alas, it has not proved to be so! It did show me, though, that it's OK, when they've done well, to praise them for it, to appreciate it, and to show them you do. It gives them more power so they can focus themselves on what they do well rather than the few (insignificant) things they do less well. It showed me, too, that my eyes are inclined to pick up those little imperfections rather than what's good.

**Correct their behaviour in a positive way**

Use positive language. For example, if they do something wrong, rather than being quick to say "no, that's wrong", suggest alternative ways they can improve their behaviour, or even better, ask <u>them</u> to suggest how they might improve their behaviour. So often I've heard parents shouting "why did you do <u>that</u>? No, no, no" with a completely disbelieving tone. I've done this myself, because it really is hard for us to understand some of the things that kids do, like the child who bails the bath out pot-full by pot-full onto the bathroom floor, or the child who just <u>has</u> to blow the candles out before the birthday-girl gets to them, and does it with such a cheeky grin of satisfaction too!

How can we use positive language? Well, I think it's OK to say 'no' to a child, but not OK to add the condemning words that tend to follow it. So instead of "no, don't do that you little rascal", maybe something like "no, let birthday-girl do it, it will be your birthday another time", or "What do you think would have been a nicer thing to do, as it's someone else's birthday?" Kids usually know when they've done wrong.

Leading by example is another positive way of teaching children about behaviour. They learn best through our example, by watching us. My son likes to do jobs around the house, only if he can get paid for it of course! When he first took on the task of mowing the lawn I have to admit the finished product fell short of perfect. There were untidy edges, numerous missed bits, grass cuttings all over the place. When he'd finished we stood together surveying it. Looking at it, it was clear that it was not good enough, so I said "do you think that's ideally how it should look?" After a few moans of protest, and after I said I wasn't paying the full price for only half a job, he got it so it was pleasing to the eye, to the standard he has seen it done before, by his dad, so he <u>had</u> known how it should have looked, but had taken the easiest option which, of course, is natural. We all like to get things done in the easiest way we can, don't we?

## Avoid negative labelling

Language is very powerful. What we say in front of our children matters. Phrases such as 'she's so....', 'he can't......', 'he doesn't like ......' are a form of label, and imply that 'that's the way they are and they won't change'. Kids hear these messages, and take them in to the point where the labels can become their identity. "Oh right, if my mum says I can't read very well, I can't."

Out of my three children, two are absolute 'professors' at technology – operating DVD and video controls and computers. The third child took longer to pick it up. She was fiddling around with the telephone the other day and whilst I stood back and watched her, a conversation started in my head – "You're not very good with technology, are you". In it's true function of 'loud speaker', my lips moved as if to speak these words out loud, I quickly shut them, whilst my brain told me that "before you're quick to make this statement, could it not be that she is perfectly capable of learning how these things work, she just may not be that interested in them".

The other mistake we can make is to make comments about our children to other adults, forgetting our child is within earshot. Kids have excellent hearing and they will listen very well, especially when the subject talked about is them! And often a comment heard from afar can have a much more powerful effect than in their immediate presence.

# Chapter 8

## WHAT ARE YOU FEEDING YOUR CHILD'S EMOTIONAL APPETITE?

If you are happy on the inside it will show on the outside. Have you noticed that when you're happy more people will smile at you or say hello to you? Likewise, in order to love others we must first love ourself. Being happy and having a positive attitude and self-esteem are more important than anything else in our lives, they are the foundations on which we and our children can build in order to do and achieve anything in our lives.

The way we think influences how we feel, our self-esteem and our achievements. When I was a child I was a very good swimmer, really good. Effortlessly I won races, especially in backstroke. I swam for a small-town team, and eventually I made it through to the County trials (a big event where we competed with the top swimmers from other teams around the County, with the aim to be picked to swim for and represent the big County team). I came second in my race, but only by a fraction of a second. I know I had it in me somewhere to win that race. I believe that if I had known then what I know now, how my beliefs and the way I think and feel about myself can affect the choices I make and my ability to do anything, who knows, I could have won that race and reached top level competitions, even the Olympics. At the time however, I had low self-esteem, negative thoughts, poor confidence, and was self-conscious about my body. I wasn't realising my full potential.

* Self-esteem (self-respect) means valuing yourself as a person. You know that you are like other people in being able to do some things

well, but not everything.  Children with self-esteem have a positive self-image and this gives them:

- Self confidence – they know that they can cope easily with the people they meet and the situations in which they find themselves.

- Self-reliance – they want to be independent.  This comes when children are encouraged to do things for themselves, eg. Babies who are allowed to feed themselves, toddlers who choose what clothes to wear, etc.

A child's self-esteem is affected by many factors, most importantly by the way the child is encouraged and supported by parents and other adults who care for him.

Other factors are:

- the child's environment, eg. Poverty and deprivation

- discrimination because of race, gender, religion

- the child may be 'different', either because of:
  - disability, eg. Deafness, lameness
  - infection, eg. HIV positive.

Self-esteem develops more strongly in children who are:

- praised for what they can do, not criticised for what they cannot do

- encouraged to develop new skills

- given choices – perhaps about the clothes they wear or toys they prefer to play with

- encouraged to discuss their feelings and express their ideas

- given minimum assistance, so allowing them to feel that they have control over their own activities.

Signs of low self-esteem may show as:

- frequently expressing dislike of herself

- trying too hard to please

- constantly belittling herself

- frequently saying that her wishes do not matter

- lack of pride in her origins

- trying to change her appearance.

* Childcare & Development , 4/e, Pamela Minett (John Murray 2001)

Having spent some time working with children who have learning difficulties, I have noticed, whilst many have particular disorders, the majority of them lack self esteem. Unfortunately there are many children who have had unstable and quite traumatic lives since birth, and many move from one foster home to another. School only serves to magnify the difficult feelings that they have. They do not believe in themselves, they believe that they cannot do the schoolwork, struggle, fail, and continue to suffer low self-esteem. It seems to be a never-ending circle.

Trying to bring these pupils through the school system and exams does not seem to be the answer. Much more emphasis needs to be put into developing and teaching systems that children can use to increase their belief in themselves and their confidence to follow what motivates them and build upon those interests. If a child does not fit into the academic requirements of the curriculum, they can be encouraged to develop their creative thinking, and find other ways they can follow their interests and be successful.

It is our relationship as parents with our children that can foster a good level of self-esteem in them. When they can love themselves they can believe in themselves, have confidence and experience more happiness, so take time to tell them you love them, sincerely, every now and then, so they feel loved and learn to love themselves. In turn, they learn to love others. If they have these strong foundations they can build on them, and achieve anything in their lives. A positive attitude is key, so that when they come across hurdles in their lives they have the confidence and persistence to overcome them.

At the same time, however, it's good for children to know that they don't have to be good at absolutely everything, and that they respect their limitations. What's important is that they're happy and have a positive self-image.

Somebody who does not love himself tends to criticise other people and is less likely to see their good points, only their faults. Likewise I've noticed the child at school who talks badly about other children has difficulty making and keeping friendships.

"My little girl had a friend who, in her company, rarely had a good word to say for their mutual friends. It was difficult for my daughter because she was friendly with all of them, but felt her loyalties divided if she went along with her. She found it difficult because she did not like hearing unkind words said about her other friends, so today they are still friends but no longer close friends".

Give them a good start from an early age by encouraging them to be <u>independent</u>, to do things for themselves. Have the patience to allow them to do this, rather than doing things for them. To be able to do things independently can give them a boost to their confidence and make their daily lives run smoothly. A child who is confident and able in everyday tasks is empowered to help other children too, and because they are so giving, they are happy to do so. I've watched 3 year olds helping other younger children and enjoying the opportunity to do so.

If a child <u>wants</u> to do something for himself, then let him. Aren't there times we don't allow our child this opportunity, and then complain later when it seems we're having to do everything for him? Young children can be encouraged to do so much for themselves, like buttering bread, dressing, putting their seatbelt on, even slicing the bread (I must admit it takes some courage with that one, especially with my 7 year-old, but she still has all her fingers!). At the Montessori pre-school my children attended, it was an everyday occurrence when children arrived with shoes on the wrong feet and strange combinations of clothes with vibrant clashing colours. What does it matter what they look like, if they're proud they chose their clothes, put them on themselves, and feel happy about it? Doing these simple things allows them to assume some responsibility, even at the smallest level, so that when they are older, bigger responsibilities can be taken on with confidence.

I sent my son at age 12 alone on the train to London (a 2 hour journey) to meet a relative there, my 10 year old daughter has cycled to the local swimming pool and gone swimming on her own (because she wanted to). Some might balk at the thought of this, and I admit at times I felt some pangs of fear, but I have the confidence to know they will act in a responsible manner, having been put in a position of responsibility. It's amazing what children will rise to when we show them we trust in them enough and are willing to give them the opportunity to be responsible.

# Chapter 9
## DISCIPLINE

I have discovered that many parents have the same discipline issues with their kids:-

- their kids bedroom is a mess and they won't clean it up.

- they won't do their homework without a fuss or a major fight.

- they play on computer games and watch TV too much.

- their kids just won't do what they say!

First and foremost, it's us parents who make the rules, and our kids need to know this! Do you 'sort of make the rules', and then back down under pressure? Kids are great at pushing the boundaries and it's a great game for them. Beware the wimp factor – are you afraid of looking the ogre if you firmly lay down the rules?

I know, you nag every now and then, and getting them to clean up their room seems impossible – it's like pushing an elephant up a hill – it would be easier to do it yourself! And that's what I found I was doing. Then I found I would get bad-tempered with them because I was resentful of the fact that it was me who was doing all the work, cleaning up after everyone else. So I decided it was time to make some changes.

How about this – <u>I let them live in a pig sty, if that's what they want!</u> Kids eventually learn that having an untidy, disorganised room means they can't find the important stuff – at that crucial last minute before leaving for school they can't find their school tie. They have to suffer the consequences of having an untidy room, on this occasion, the consequence being detention after school for not having full school uniform. Bearing the consequences of their behaviour is how they learn. It is not wise to help them to look for that lost item at the last moment, because you're bailing them out! And they won't learn.

And of course it comes to the hour for homework, when the child is forced to sit at the table, with parent bright red, veins bursting through frustration, wondering why his child won't just get on, do it, and get it over with! At times like this, when your last drop of patience has gone, you wonder at the meaning of homework – can it be useful if it's this destructive to your home life?

If this is happening then stop rather than force them. If they don't do their homework, they have to take the punishment at school, and most kids are fully aware of what the punishment will be.

We often push our kids to do these things to avoid our own (parents') embarrassment. If our kids don't do their homework it will look bad on us, we'll be branded bad parents. If they don't tidy their room, what will people visiting think of us?

I do believe that our children are their own people. Life is about taking responsibility for ourselves, and it starts with things like homework and bedrooms. Accepting responsibility at an early age means kids develop the right attitude for adulthood. In society today, people who refuse to accept responsibility for their own actions and lives tend to blame outside influences or other people for how their lives are going, don't take control of their own lives, and become victims. They are people who don't have power and don't believe they have the power to direct their own lives.

A good question to ask yourself is "Is your child's behaviour a reflection of how you're dealing with him?" Remember, a good relationship through talking, listening, time, patience and setting a good example, builds respect. If a child respects you they will be more likely to respond to your disciplinary rules. All kids will, of course, push the boundaries, and that's natural. They wouldn't be kids if they didn't. Accept that kids will be kids, whatever they get up to, and most of all, forget worrying and thinking your kids are an exception by what they get up to. You can be sure there are millions of kids doing just the same all over the world! And most of all, let us be able to laugh about it later!

Picture this: A boy age 6 and girl age 3. His favourite hobby is to wind her up as much as possible, and today he just won't let up. His jibes whip her fiery nature into a blaze like a blow torch to a gas holder. Mum and dad are downstairs, they can hear the familiar sound of distant screaming, and climb the stairs to investigate what's happening. In disbelief they discover the girl with a broken glass in her hand (one from mum's best collection) and the boy whimpering 'help'. It was just like a scene from a bar brawl in a western. In her rage she had broken a glass over the back of his head! You could say he got more than he deserved that day! Luckily we were able to pick a large piece of glass out of his head, and he was OK.

This is a true story, and we still laugh about it!

*"Remember, as far as anyone knows, we're a nice normal family"*
Homer Simpson

**Here are some more rules to discipline that I have found to be invaluable:-**

**Be a good example to your kids by obeying your own rules** – kids are quick to point out when you don't, and will use that to undermine your authority. You are their role model. OK, yes, they may have other role models, but really it's you who's their key role model, so if you swear, guess what, no matter how much you tell <u>them</u> not to, they will – it's not "do as I say" but "do as I do".

This one comes up for me almost everyday. When I remind my kids to put their plates in the dishwasher, I get "but daddy didn't". When I remind them to put their shoes in the shoe cupboard, I get "but you haven't".

"On a quick trip to the supermarket today I saw a couple browsing the shelves and at the same time having a conversation. The dad swore every swear word I've ever heard, and in front of their young son too. I wonder, isn't it likely his son will be doing the same himself, if not already?"

**Think before being too harsh or overbearing** – especially with teenagers, they are sensitive to the fairness of your rules and punishments. If you are seen as being unfair rebellion takes over, and you may lose their respect. I know this is a tough one. I have found that my reaction to a blatant refusal or off-hand response is to immediately impose a harsh restriction, through my anger. This does only make things worse, and I learnt that it's best to take a deep breath and consider a more realistic answer, rather than to change it when I've 'cooled down'.

Sometimes we find it hard to understand our kids, to see the world from their perspective, through their eyes, and this can mean we just can't comprehend nor accept their behaviour. This example from a mum might help:-

"My 3 sons can be aggressive with each other both physically and verbally. Being one of 3 girls I have found it hard to witness how boys play. They seem to jump all over each other. It's not just my sons but also when they have friends over they all pile on top as well. Even my husband gets stuck in with it. I read a very helpful book by Steve Biddulph called 'Raising Boys' which advised that this is normal behaviour for boys and it helps them discover what is acceptable and what is not acceptable physically. I do wonder though if they do ever learn, especially as my husband clearly has not as yet!"

**Be consistent** – saying 'no' to something one day, and 'yes' to it the next isn't being consistent. I've found kids have extra sensitivity where this is concerned. It's at the time when you are not consistent that their amazingly good memory comes into it's own. They can remember two years ago at the barbeque (when you were in the middle of some juicy gossip with your friend) when you said they <u>could</u> kick the football over the roof, so why can't they now?

I believe that our word is all-important. People are less likely to respect someone who says they'll do something and then doesn't, ie. breaks their word. After a few let-downs they're unlikely to trust that person, they won't believe they mean what they say, and may be less likely themselves to stick to <u>their</u> word with that person, thinking, 'oh well, it's OK if I don't turn up, he's always doing that, he'll understand'. The truth is, most of us know someone like that. It doesn't necessarily mean we like that person less, but we don't perhaps respect him or rely on him when there's an issue that's important to us.

Kids though, do have an absolute trust in their parents, and will notice and follow their parents' example. They are sensitive too, to our word, if we all too easily say 'no' to something and then back down, or, and this is a tough one, if we say we'll take them somewhere, and don't follow through! Perhaps we have to think very carefully before we make promises, even with little things, so we're sure we can follow through.

One evening all the members of our family were getting ready to go out. My son, who was shifting into teenager at the time, didn't want to come. It was imperative, on this occasion, that he came with us. After much argument, and realising we wouldn't relent, he shut and locked himself in the bathroom. He wouldn't come out, so his dad said in clear terms, if you don't come out I'll break the door down. I reminded him that, if we're doing our 'sticking to our word' thing, he'll have to follow-through with his threat, should it come to it. Well, time was ticking and we had to go, so after one more warning, he still wasn't moving (it's that teenage determination) my husband, in true Hollywood movie style, broke through the door (it wasn't difficult). The door catch broke and a shard of wood flew past my son's ear as he sat on the side of the bath. Wow! I don't know who was more shocked – him or me. I suppose it wasn't the ideal way of getting the message across (and I'm not recommending it to you), but it was a pretty clear way. The message: Dad sticks to his word.

I've found it's a good idea to get some rules agreed with my husband so there are no inconsistencies between us. Of course this isn't always possible, because new situations are coming up everyday, and there's always one of us who's indecisive, that's usually me, so I often say "ask your dad". I'm sure someone out there may identify with this!

**Find out what their motivation is**, for example, if it's money, and they're persistently misbehaving, the threat of withdrawal of an amount of their pocket money could be effective. For very young children their motivation might be the feeling of a sense of achievement, or approval, so praise has great significance to them, and we've all heard of reward systems where stars are awarded for good behaviour, with a prize or gift awarded on the target number of stars met. Young children also like to feel included, so if they are misbehaving, a time to 'cool off', ie. step out of the situation, be it a party or a game, can be useful.

For older children, money is a common motivation, but for many it may be time at the computer, time with friends or outings to favourite places. With discipline like this I've found the tough bit is actually sticking to it. Sometimes, if only my son had that pocket money he would stop nagging me for money, or if my daughter could go to her friend's house I'd at least have some peace! So it's easy to give in, and then days or weeks later I wonder why my warnings are not having much effect.

This is a really common complaint amongst parents – that their kids just don't do as they say. It's really about being tough, and sticking to your rules, no matter how many complaints, guilt tactics "you don't love me", "all my other friends have <u>nice</u> parents", you get. And the disputes seem to last a long time – but it's worth it overall if you just hang in there.

**Work things out with your partner**, by consistently showing respect for one another. Kids watch how you treat each other and follow your example, so if you're not being respectful towards your partner it undermines that person's authority, and your kids will think it's OK for them to do so too. My husband used to pick me up on things he didn't agree with, just little things say, in the kitchen. The kids would hear and would say "Yeah, see mum?". I pointed this out to him, and he agreed not to mention things in front of them, and what's more, he agreed to overlook those little things too!

If you are separated from your partner, and still speaking to each other, you can try to do this too. If you don't particularly meet up and spend time together, at least be respectful about your partner when talking about him or her in front of your children.

**Stick at it!**

A dear friend of mine, who has much experience working with families as a Health Visitor said this:-

"In my experience it is all too easy to give up if a new method of dealing with behaviour does not work the first, second or third time. It is really important to pursue your decision and keep at it. Sleeping problems are an excellent example. It may take not days but weeks of leaving a child to cry instead of picking them up during the night. For most children it is a habit which parents have reinforced. Most children come to no harm if left to cry for up to 2 hours. It sounds harsh, but it really is being cruel to be kind. The child and the parents all need their sleep and sleep deprivation can be so hard to cope with".

I'm sure many will agree. When I had my first introduction to the world of 'zombie parenthood', I recall saying "I could cope with absolutely anything if only I had some sleep".

Above all, though, remember, the perfect parent doesn't exist. He or she only exists in dreams and ideals. Forgive me for saying this, but we're just never going to be perfect, given the challenges we face daily. Likewise then, how can we expect our kids to be perfect? Accept that they won't always get things right, and that often the best lessons learnt are those learnt the hard way, that is, learning by our mistakes and the consequences. Like us, they learn that there are always consequences to their behaviour. For example, a teenager I know, who had a job delivering the local free newspaper, for weeks he didn't deliver all of them, but dumped them down a side alley. The delivery company discovered what was happening and, of course, dropped him from their employment. The consequence was, he had no extra money to buy the pro skateboard he wanted and the clothes he wanted. When his money ran out, he learnt the hard way, through the consequences of his behaviour.

And this is often how most children learn best, because no matter how much we <u>tell</u> them how to be, what to do, or warn them what will happen if ..., they won't take our advice, they'll go right ahead and do it <u>their</u> way!

A boy close to me (13 years old) one day did a very foolish thing. The boys who he hung around with on a regular basis thought it would be a good idea to call at the house when he was alone there and his parents were out. They rang the doorbell and then ran away, more times than he could take. After a while he lost his temper, took a large kitchen knife and strode up the road to where the gang were loitering. In his temper, he then threatened one of the boys with the knife. He did not use the knife, but his actions had the victim quite frightened as he thought that he just might be attacked, and he ran off.

The consequence of this behaviour, however, was that the gang of boys, with whom he had previously walked to school with every morning, shunned him, relayed the story of the knife to everyone they could, thus giving him a bad name, and continually picked on him and made fun of him from then on. He spent several weeks quite alone, both physically and emotionally, and regretted his behaviour. It would have been quite easy for his parents to step in, talk to the gang about their unreasonable behaviour ringing the doorbell, picking on him, shunning him, but they didn't. Instead he learnt a lot from the incident. He learnt to think before he reacts, he learnt the power of his emotions and actions, that there are consequences to his actions, that there are always two sides to every story (his side being that he was taunted unreasonably, the gang's side that he overreacted without reason). He learnt what it is like to have no friends. He learnt what it is like to be bullied. He ultimately also learnt how to defend himself, the art of patience, and how to stand up for himself and to stop the bullying. And best of all, he learnt that they weren't the most ideal friends he could have had because out of this event he found a set of new friends who did not look for or take part in any trouble.

It's often painful and frustrating for the parent to have to watch their child make mistakes and suffer the consequences, possibly time and time again, until they learn, but it really is the best way. It gets the message in loud and clear.

Anyway, it may be a consolation to know that anything that goes wrong is just a 'blip' in the graph of life. In later years all concerned will look back and either flinch a little with embarrassment, or just laugh, and when we have the benefit of hindsight we see that many things happen for the better, that something good comes out of times of adversity.

**Relax!**

Most of our worries in parenting come from our expectation that we must be perfect. We worry that if we don't get it right our kids will grow up to be social misfits, unsuccessful, or unhappy. Part of this is that we want to look good. If our kids don't meet expectations of society it looks bad on us.

The ability to let go of these expectations, especially when there is really very little alternative, and love and accept our children for who they are – individuals, is valuable and freeing. These words from a mother of a 15 year old boy provide a useful illustration:-

"When your children get older they do not necessarily become the people you expected they would. My oldest son is extremely lazy. He is very clever and could get A stars for his GCSE's if he put any work in. However, he is happy to get 5 A - C's and so does very little work. He would much rather go and kick a football around with his mates than do homework or revision. As his mum, I find this really difficult to accept. I feel he should be working his hardest and doing his best. I'm sure that's what we have told him time and time again. My son feels he does not need to do his best, just what he feels is adequate. Maybe he will become a very contented adult because he will not put too many demands on himself".

I believe that a loving and secure home is the most significant ingredient in the life of a child, and that if we can do our best with the other stuff, then that's great, but keep our focus on caring for our family relationships and fostering a good environment at home.

I hope I have been able to connect with you in this chapter in showing how our relationships shape our family life. I really do think it is the key. It isn't easy, when we take into account our day to day responsibilities, and the thing to remember is that nobody's perfect.

The next part of this book is about changes we made in our family life that helped our relationships considerably. I'm not saying that you must make these changes, but I want to illustrate how fundamental they have been to us, and why.

It involved changing our priorities with regards to our time and space, and challenging some conventional ways of life that seem to commonly go un-challenged.

# Chapter 10

## WHERE DO YOUR PRIORITIES LIE? AT HOME OR OUTSIDE?

Strong families make it a priority to spend time together. Take time to make time to be a family together by making space in your busy schedules. It's really easy to forget time for 'us'. The only way to do this is to make it a priority – perhaps put it in your diary, or write it on the kitchen noticeboard as a reminder!

Perhaps the rule of the house should be that every member should be home at a particular time of the day. I know you may be saying that this is totally impossible in your household, and this is understandable, especially with maybe both parents working, or one parent working till late. Endeavouring to bring everyone together at least once or twice during the working week would be better than not at all.

> *"The table is the most important item of furniture for a good family life – much more important than the sofa".*
> Alison, Mum of 2 boys, Worthing, England

I have a friend who teaches Interior Design at a local college. One of the tasks that she sets for her students during the year is that of designing an area for eating. One year, when the class were discussing and planning the task, it emerged that hardly any of the students ate around the table at home. Members of their families ate at different times of the day, sitting on the sofa in front of the television, eating previously cooked dinners that had been reheated in the microwave.

If we sit around a table, conversation is sure to happen. Everybody's facing each other, they're not distracted by other tasks, and everyone is present and part of the event. The dining-table becomes the field on which all sorts of emotions (pleasure, guilt, anger, happiness) are played out, and children learn about the connections between food, feelings and family life. This is where parents can find out about what's been going on in their children's lives. The answer to "what did you do at school?" is less likely to be met with "nothing" at the dinner table. It's a good place for children to learn about things too. There's more opportunity to answer those complicated questions that come up, those questions that require more than two minutes grabbed while putting our coats on and rushing out of the door.

Parents, take moments of complete quiet, where you are free to think and relax without interruption or noise pollution. It's vital in order to re-charge your batteries, both physically and mentally.

> *"Of one thing I am certain, the body is not the measure of healing – peace is the measure".*
>
> George Melton

I don't think we slow down enough, probably because time is at a premium and we try to cram as much as possible in to our dwindling spare time. I visited a zoo recently with my children and, at a rare moment of space and no crowds (the place was heaving with people that day), I watched a pair of servals (wild cats). There was something quite fascinating going on between them, the larger cat following its companion, and the other retaliating with scowls. I stood for quite a while, taking in their interaction. Lots of people stopped whilst I was there, pointed out the cats to their children, but no-one stopped long enough to notice what was going on. I think we miss so much because we do not just stop and observe. If we did so, both adults and children, we would gain far more pleasure and learn so much more from our environment.

**Take relaxing holidays**

After the experiences of crowded airports, crowded beaches and, well, crowds, we now take holidays 'closer to nature'. A recent favourite for us is a cottage (named Gilfach Goch, in a little village called Llanbedr, in Wales, www.holidaycottagewales.co.uk). It is a remote farm, near woods, streams, Snowdonia mountains, and the seaside. We go on frequent walks through woods, where the kids can play in the streams and waterfalls, and where they can appreciate nature, something we believe is important that they will carry with them into adulthood. I remember as a child my mum taking me on long walks with her, and I recall moaning for most of the way, but as an adult I treasure those memories, and I can still smell the flowers and woods in summer and winter, and appreciate those experiences, and they have helped me realise the difference between the two worlds – the natural world and man-made world. The natural world is all about peace. When you come to the end of that footpath through the woods though, and reach the busy road (the man-made world), the contrast is so clear to see.

Children do not necessarily need fair rides and attractions to have fun. Simple things can be just as much fun, and longer lasting, especially in their memories. They love climbing trees, building dams and sailing toy boats in streams. They love adventure games in the woods, finding insects, making sandcastles and forts at the beach, catching crabs and rock-pooling – how often do we do these activities nowadays?

I do, however, understand that these activities are not easily accessible to everybody, but urge you to consider a break away like this once in a while or whenever possible. Parks are wonderful places to go to on a regular basis. A full day, with a picnic, will enable your child to be absorbed in the environment and to devise imaginative games to play.

**Buy more time**

A friend said to me the other day "I wish I didn't have to work so I could have more time for my kids". Being a working mum is one of the hardest and most admirable jobs in the world. Not only is there the responsibility at work, but at home as well, and all the other tasks (cooking, cleaning, washing, ironing) you have to do as well. We sat down and considered that, in order to work full-time, she had to buy a second car, buy two sets of clothes (work and home), buy more expensive convenience foods, pay for childcare, and pay more tax. She realised that in the long run, with all the added extras, working full-time could be costing her more than, say, working part-time or working from home!

# Chapter 11

## WHOSE PRINCIPLES REALLY CONTROL YOUR FAMILY LIFE? YOURS OR A STRANGER'S?

**Television**

If you want to shatter that peaceful world, turn on the TV. I cannot see what's so great about it. It's true, there are some good things on TV. TV can be educational, informative, and entertaining. But how much of that good quality TV does your family actually watch? When you get home and 'switch on', are you channel flicking and watching what just happens to be on at that moment, or are you planning your viewing and being selective about what you watch? What I found in our household was that we were channel flicking and watching poor quality programmes. It was a typical case of knowing what we should be doing - planning our viewing, but this just wasn't happening. This didn't work out to be practical in our daily life. We realised something needed to be done.

I tried restricting the times we watched TV to certain times of the day, but this did not work out. Each day had it's own commitments, with clubs or outings, and there was not a 'TV watching time' that fitted in. Thus, time was 'made up' at other times of the day, the argument being "mum, we didn't have our TV time this afternoon, so can we watch it now?" If the answer was 'no', then all hell let loose and a family argument ensued. Also, time watching TV gradually extended, either because the movie they were watching went on longer than expected, or because I was busy, and it was handy to have no interruptions and get on with what I wanted to do. So, restricting times didn't work out.

TV took the fun and interest out of other activities. No matter what the activity, whether it be going to a club, seeing a friend, or even everyday tasks, like doing homework, having a bath, going to bed, eating dinner, there was always SOMETHING on the box. TV seemed to control their minds, and controlled our family life.

Secondly, I began to question some of the messages that were coming through 'the box'. The lack of morals in television content was apparent, with sexual innuendos on children's Saturday morning television shows, programmes about family conflicts, shows where unruly children were controlling their parents' lives, where parental values were persistently challenged. Now, I'm no great moralist, but I did notice that this kind of material has increased considerably since the time I was watching TV as a kid, and I do believe that prolonged viewing of such material does, in the end, make it an everyday, acceptable way of behaving to the viewer. The more it is watched, the more we become acclimatised to it, and the less we are aware of its effects. I really believe that what we feed our mind on is crucial to the environment of our mind. If, say, we watch a lot of news or crime programmes with all their content about murders, wars, rape and burglary, we are feeding our mind on fear. I find it ironic that, at the end of a topical crime programme in the UK, after we've seen the horrific crimes that have been happening in real life, and heard about the criminals out loose on the streets who are Wanted, the presenter says "Now, don't have nightmares, sleep well tonight"!

So what did we do in our household?

We made the decision to 'switch off' the TV, so that we could not receive incoming broadcasted programmes, but that we could still watch DVDs of our choice. This seemed quite a big change to make at the time, but actually doing it did not cause major difficulties for anyone in the family. I myself did find it difficult adjusting to spending my evenings reading rather than watching television and eating chocolates! My eldest child was the one who found it the most difficult to adjust. For about 3 months he wandered around the house, with nothing to do, apart from annoying his sisters, or hanging around me in the kitchen. I admit I did occasionally wonder about the wisdom of what I had done, but in time, with much patience, it paid off. He started to find other things to do. Despite being 'allergic' to books, he did start reading them, not very much, but it was better than none! He found things to research on the internet, and he developed a healthy interest in martial arts, a sport which we all had recently taken up, practising it at home. Previously having been a 'foggy' thinker, he displayed clearer thinking patterns. He enjoyed a conversation a little more often, talking to me, rather than living in a world of his own with only a grunt to converse. My daughters whinged for a few days, and then it appeared they had forgotten television was gone. They happily played lots of imaginative games together, and still do to this day.

You may be thinking how could I have done this, it's cruel, kids should be able to make their own choice. Well, I don't believe it's cruel, not when I believe it to be something for their benefit. As I said, they can watch DVDs and films of their choice, and there's no shortage of those. The main benefit, and I don't think they've missed it at all, is the elimination of constant 'noise' and low quality stuff that is drip-fed constantly when the TV is on. They <u>do</u> have a choice – from better quality films.

Since implementing this change in our home, I'm pretty sure that there is a strong connection with obesity and the amount of TV people watch. If we get a DVD to watch, the automatic reaction is to get a snack, and 'munch' right through it!

For those sceptical about throwing out their TV, take a look at some of the facts.

Barbara J Brock, Professor of Recreation Management, Eastern Washington University, conducted a National Survey in America in February and March 2000, and presented her results on www. tvturnoff.org. She says that 98% of American adults spend 40% of their leisure time sitting and watching TV. She carried out a survey in order to find out about the small proportion of Americans that don't watch TV, to find out who they are, why they turned the TV off and what makes them tick. Her results are fascinating. Here's a few points she found about TV free families who responded:-

**There are three common themes of why families have made the choice to turn the TV off:-**

1. To regain and retain a closeness of family.

2. To place a small measure of control on what children are exposed to in the four walls of their homes.

3. To stimulate dreams and creativity in themselves and their children.

Most respondents simply decided to take back some time for family in a busy world by getting rid of the TV. They were frustrated with poor programs, violence, and commercialism or identified family communication or discipline problems. Some respondents came from homes literally saturated with TV for most of their own childhood and adult lives. Many negative memories were harboured about being left out, ignored, or lack of interaction as a family. These respondents chose to live and raise their families in a completely different manner than the one in which they were brought up. Others were from homes where TV was not owned or severely restricted. Looking back, they liked this lifestyle and continued the tradition. The final group never really made a conscious decision to not own a TV, rather were too busy to buy one in young adult years and found they liked their lives that way, especially with children.

**Results of switching the TV off?**

- They have about an hour of meaningful conversation per **day** with their children (national average is 38 minutes per **week**).

- They come from all walks of life, income brackets, levels of education, races etc. Most are in their 30s, married with 2 children, two thirds have religious affiliations and 41% send their kids to public schools (private and home school equally divided the rest).

- 92% of parents say their children "never or rarely" complain about the lack of TV or pressure them to buy brand names and popular toys.

- As to their children's heroes, most votes went for mum and dad. Others include teachers, Harry Potter, Jesus, Martin Luther King, grandparents and Michael Jordan.

- 80% feel their marriages are stronger due to no TV – more cuddle time.

- They are readers (adults and children). Get the majority

of their news from newspapers, and a few national magazines.

- They (kids and adults) rarely feel they're missing out – totally on the gain side.

- More than half of their children get all A's in school.

- The computer does **not** take over the role of TV in most homes. Though 98% own a computer, only 1-3 hours of recreational use per week was reported by adults. (When asked if their children use the computer more or less than kids who watch TV, nearly half felt their children use it less due to the passive nature of the activity).

- Children entertain themselves and play for long hours with fewer sibling fights. 70% of parents felt their children got along better with no TV.

- One family with an ADD child reported removing TV from the home (under the paediatrician's advice) – the child blossomed and took tremendous strides in development.

One comment from a survey participant sums it up "We have not watched TV for more than 16 years, not out of a statement against society or any overt religious injunction, but a simple desire to have TIME for a more meaningful marriage and family in the face of a busy life".

Some practical advice: if you can live through 20 minutes of whining, your children **will** find something to do!

The TV turnoff website, www.tvturnoff.org gives tips for turning the TV off, and suggestions for coping.

Barbara J Brock's recent book "Living Outside The Box" gives much more detail about her national survey, and sets out to answer the question 'Why is it that now, when we in America have more leisure time at our disposal than ever before, we so often feel we have less and less? Could the ever-expanding role of television in our lives be part of the explanation?' Her book can be obtained from Amazon.com or the East Washington University press www.ewu.edu/ewupress

Parents, children who do not watch television, and along with it, commercials, do not badger their parents for the latest gismos and toys!

No TV means <u>peace</u>. Peace means lots of time for conversation, thought, reading, and creativity. No peace means no space for conversation, thought, reading and creativity.

Time spent watching television not only takes away from important activities such as reading, school work, playing, exercise, family interaction, and social development, but children also learn information from television that may be inappropriate or incorrect. They often cannot tell the difference between the fantasy presented on television and reality. They are influenced by the thousands of commercials seen each year, many of which are for alcohol, junk food, fast foods, and toys.

Children who watch a lot of television are likely to:

- Have lower grades in school

- Read fewer books

- Have problems with attention

- Exercise less

- Be overweight

Violence, sexuality, race and gender stereotypes, and drug and alcohol abuse are all common themes of television programmes. Young children are impressionable and may assume that what they see on television is typical, safe, and acceptable. As a result, television also exposes children to behaviours and attitudes that may be overwhelming and difficult to understand.

Take, for example, the broadcasting of <u>News</u>. Children often see or hear the news many times a day through television, radio, newspapers, magazines, and the Internet. Seeing and hearing about local and world events, such as natural disasters, catastrophic events, and crime reports, may cause children to experience stress, anxiety, and fears.

There have also been several changes in how news is reported that have given rise to the increased potential for children to experience negative effects. These changes include the following:

- television channels and Internet services and sites which report the news 24 hours a day

- television channels broadcasting live events as they are unfolding, in "real time"

- increased reporting of the details of the private lives of public figures and role models

- pressure to get news to the public as part of the competitive nature of the entertainment industry

- detailed and repetitive visual coverage of natural disasters and violent acts

The possible negative effects of news can be lessened by parents, teachers, or other adults by watching the news with the child and talking about what has been seen or heard. The child's age, maturity, developmental level, life experiences, and vulnerabilities should guide how much and what kind of news the child watches.

The American Academy of Child and Adolescent Psychiatry suggests that studies of the effects of TV violence on children and teenagers have found that children may:

- become "immune" to the horror of violence

- gradually accept violence as a way to solve problems

- imitate the violence they observe on television, and

- identify with certain characters, victims and/or victimizers

They also suggest that extensive viewing of television violence by children causes them to be more aggressive, and that even watching just one violent programme can increase their aggressiveness. Children are more likely to copy very realistic violent shows, especially if they are not punished for it, and children with emotional, behavioural, learning or impulse control problems may be more easily influenced by TV violence.

The American Academy of child and adolescent psychiatry gives some advice on how parents can take steps to minimise the effects of watching News scenes with their children, and to protect them from excessive TV violence. For further information, The American Academy of Child and Adolescent Psychiatry website is www.aacap. org.

Media violence is so pervasive in our lives, and comes in so many different contexts and styles, that it is impossible to make accurate generalizations about its real-world effects based on experiments in the laboratory, or statistical correlations between media viewing and aggressive behaviour. Despite the claims of some psychologists and politicians, the actual results from social science research into the effects of media violence have been weak.

It is clear that the mass media have profound effects on our attitudes and behaviour, but it depends on the different ways that it is presented, and the personality, background, intelligence and life experiences of the person watching it. As to our personal lives, it is up to the individual to make their own judgement. For more information, and a broader picture, there are some website addresses included on the references page at the back of this book.

It's a novelty for kids to get to watch adult movies. My kids have on occasion come home from friends' houses to proudly tell me they watched an adult movie. It is difficult to gauge what effect these experiences have on them, but from my own experience, I know that when I was too young I watched the movie 'Jaws'. After that, despite being a strong swimmer I was afraid of swimming in deep water, not because of the fear of drowning, but the fear of what was beneath!

One year, a friend of mine, in her role as college tutor, had a student in her class who was self-harming. One day, when she was at her lowest ebb, she confided in her tutor for some comfort and advice because she was almost suicidal and didn't know what to do. After much conversation and questioning, when all the emotion and confusion had been worked through, it turned out the problem was that her mum never switched off the TV! Her mum wasn't talking to her. All she wanted was her mum's attention, like the past times when they had played family games of Monopoly around the table. She just wanted her time.

Turn off the TV? You have a choice. Personally, I recommend it. It creates peace in the home, it creates opportunities for meaningful time together. It eliminates pressure from commercials for toys, junk foods, drugs, and moreover it allows kids the space for creative play and other activities that stimulate their imagination.

You may be asking, by not watching TV, <u>would my kids feel left-out</u> when with their peers? People love to talk about TV, and if you don't watch it, it is a bit of a conversation-stopper! But I can reassure you that my kids don't suffer any adverse social effects as a result of not watching TV, and this is how they deal with it. If when with friends they are discussing TV, they <u>ask questions</u> about it – that way they're showing an interest, and, of course, their friends love to tell them about it!

**Some statistics:-**

* In a Time Magazine Poll (03.02.05) 53% of respondents said that they think the FCC should place stricter controls on broadcast-channel shows depicting sex and violence. 68% believe the entertainment industry has lost touch with viewers' moral standards. 66% said there is too much violence on open-air TV. 58% said too much cursing and 50% said there is too much sexual content on TV.

* Average time kids spend watching TV each day – 4 hours.

* Children spend more time watching television than in any other activity except sleep (Huston and Wright, University of Kansas. "Television and Socialization of Young Children")

* 54% of kids have a TV in their bedroom.

* 44% of kids say they watch something different when they're alone than with their parents.

* 66% of children (ages 10 to 16) surveyed say that their peers are influenced by TV shows.

* 62% say that sex on TV shows and movies influences kids to have sex when they are too young.

* 77% say there is too much sex before marriage on television.

* 65% say that shows like The Simpsons and Married...With Children, encourage kids to disrespect parents.

* A majority of parents say they are "very" concerned about the amount of sex (60%) and violence (53%) their children are exposed to on TV.

* 86% of Britons feel their government should step in to regulate sexually explicit television and magazine images aimed at children, according to a BBC poll of more than 1,000 people. While the strongest support came from 55 to 64 year-olds (92%), a surprising 78% of 18 to 24 year-olds also believe tougher restrictions are necessary to discourage adolescent sex. Britain is currently experiencing a surge in STDs (up 57% from 1995) and HIV cases (up 20% from last year), along with a rising rate of teenage pregnancies {Telegraph.co.uk, 9/7/04 stats}.

**Computers and Video Games**

This is a technological age. More and more, kids are living in a 'virtual world', and less and less they are playing simple games that stimulate imagination. The owner of the farm holiday cottage we visit remarked upon his observations of some children who visit – children who don't know <u>how</u> to play on a farm, in a natural 'playground' – it's an alien land to them!

There are mixed feelings on the subject of playing on computers and video games. Like anything, it's OK in moderation. Internet games come in thousands of different shapes and forms. The internet has good and bad, but just like television, <u>it's a good idea to keep an eye on what your kids are doing.</u>

The problem in our house was that our son could happily play all day long on the computer, and then when asked to turn it off, would fly into a wild rage about how unreasonable I was being, and 'can I have 5 more minutes?' A bit like the television, there was never a good time to switch it off. Games become real too. One game on the internet involves building a room in a virtual hotel, creating your own character, and moving around conversing with other characters, with other real people behind them. It's imperative that you make your child aware of the dangers of giving out their personal information to any of these virtual characters, but if you are going to allow your child to play these games, I suppose there is some element of risk you have to take. Kids are very innocent to worldly dangers, and if someone wants to con them out of their personal details they will find any way to do it. My daughter innocently gave away her password to another virtual person, and subsequently this person stole her account, her character and her room with its furniture inside. She had in effect become a victim of crime, and told me she wasn't ever going to play on that game again. She was quite upset. These games can also involve spending money and offer varied ways of paying. My son paid through his mobile phone, and I discovered that he was paying monthly to be a member of a club. It is the addictive nature of these games that encourages them to pay monthly. Their friends are also playing these games. They can play with their friends on the internet, without going to their homes! I'm not saying that kids should not play these games, but that for some kids it is addictive and they can spend a lot of time staring at a screen rather than doing other worthwhile activities.

I was quite shocked to see a large advert for a virtual world game, on the stairs at a High School! Are schools and the Government encouraging it? It appears so, or are they getting paid for displaying the advert, and money is more important?

Plenty of research on the effects of video games has been carried out.

Dr. Steve Dorman, professor of health and kinesiology, along with colleagues at the University of Florida, examined kids and video games and concluded that some kids can become dangerously close to being addicted to them, can be affected by them mentally and can even suffer physical ailments requiring medical treatment. He says that video games can induce seizures in some children. The flashing of lights and the photosensitivity of the images from the screen can trigger a seizure-like occurrence, in some children who are already prone to such seizures.

"They may provoke a seizure more often than watching a television program because of the way the images are projected on the screen, plus children sit closer to a video screen than they do to a television set," Dorman explains. Treatment for such seizures requires avoidance of the video games or anticonvulsant drugs, he says.

"Physicians have a term for a seizure caused by video games. They refer to it as 'dark warrior epilepsy," adds Dorman.  Many video games require repeated clicking and pressing of buttons on a control monitor, adds Dorman. The injury is called nintendinitis and occurs when there is severe pain in the tendon of the thumb.

"Again, the only cure is to abstain from playing video games for several days," says Dorman.

Aggression levels of kids playing video games has been a debated topic, Dorman adds. "Playing a video game seems to lead children to exhibit behaviours similar to those portrayed in the game," he notes.

"Violent video games may arouse children in the same way as violent television cartoons. We need further research in this area, but studies show that children tend to model what they experience in video games."

Dorman says, however, that <u>there are some positive results from video games.</u>

Video games can enhance certain skills in a child. For example, he cites "spatial visualization" - the ability to rotate mentally and twist two and three-dimensional objects - can improve in children by playing video games.

"Students with a high degree of spatial visualization are usually high achievers in maths and science," he points out. Occupations which require mechanical tasks or machinery operation also demand high spatial visualization skills, he says.

But one drawback to video games is their effect on how kids learn. Dorman says some evidence exists that kids who view video games want all learning to take a "gaming" approach. In other words, it must be fun.

"It has given rise to 'edutainment' media," Dorman says. "It is software that resembles video-game type learning materials. "Video games are not going away," he adds. "They are here to stay. We should pay attention to the content of these games and their effects on children. It is important for health promoters to understand how this technology can be used to improve health. For example, using these games may provide a way to improve health in children and adults who live in an increasing technologically-based society."

More information on research studies on the effects of video games can be found at www.mediafamily.org

In our home, what I've found is that because we have just one computer available it is not possible for each child to spend long amounts of time in front of the screen. The computer is also situated in a communal room, the dining room, rather than in a child's bedroom. This means that not only do they spend shorter amounts of time on it, they can't get up in the night to play it.

# Chapter 12

## SCHOOL

Why do I mention school? Well, it's where our kids spend 5 days a week in the care of others, to 'better themselves', to socialise, and it can be a great source of worry for parents. We've been conditioned to put too much importance on 'education'. The result can be that school issues, homework tasks, our child's performance at school, can put pressure on us as parents because we need to feel that our children are doing well. I totally support the idea of education as one of the ways to achievement in life, but I don't see it as the only means to success. I believe that self-esteem, a strong belief in ourselves and the confidence and motivation to succeed are just as important.

This is why I changed my perspective on school.

**Children develop at different ages**

All children are different, and they learn in different ways and at different speeds. Some children adapt well to the academic environment, some learn best through play, some through practical lessons, some are good at getting their ideas onto paper, some are best at drawing, and some at projecting their ideas through speech, music and drama. If your child is not fitting in perfectly at school, or achieving what is expected, it's not necessarily a reason to worry. School is an institution with it's own set of rules, it's own set routine, and children are expected to fit into it. This, of course, is totally alien to the young, excitable, free-will of a child, and it takes some adjusting to!

Because of the way the curriculum is structured, all kids are required to keep up with what's going on. If your son or daughter is having difficulty keeping up, this can lead to frustration and loss of self-esteem. The Government sets targets that all schools are expected to meet, so be aware the school's aims are to meet those targets. Some kids are slow starters at school. A parent may worry about this, and think there is something wrong with their child because he or she is not reading at the same level as the other children in the class, and may feel a compulsion to push him too young with his reading. Avoid putting pressure on, because – all kids learn when they are ready to learn, and just because they do not fit into the academic mould expected of them, this does not mean there is something wrong.

Here's a story from a mum who was worried about her son's development at school:-

"When my son was seven years old he was having real difficulty learning reading skills. Simple words like cat, phonically spoken (ie using the letter sounds 'c-a-t', he could not even hear, let alone read.

I thought there was something wrong with him. The other children in the class seemed to be doing well, some of them already on simple reading books. I worried about this a lot, and I admit, I did push him, but got nowhere. So I just gave up, and did not push him, nor pressurise him into learning his spellings, because it was doing more harm than good. Then, a year and a half later, at a parents evening, his teacher remarked "Isn't his reading coming along well?" I did not admit that I'd given up, but I did admit that I had not seen him bring a reading book home for a long time and, well, he's just not interested in reading. I discovered that he was reading paperbacks, and this through reading at school and no practice at home! If only I'd known not to worry, I would have saved myself a lot of grey hairs!"

Today too many labels are given to people. Unfortunately the label "learning disabled" or "dyslexic" does not help the bearer because if you feel certain that you are "learning disabled" or "dyslexic" it becomes a self-fulfilling prophecy, a belief that that's the way you are, and implies that it is an unchangeable and permanent problem! Whatever the difficulty, is it really something to focus on? After all, people like Winston Churchill, Richard Branson, Einstein were all dyslexic. They did not do well at school, but were/are amazing and successful people. In fact, Einstein was a poor student, preferring day-dreaming to studying, and was eventually expelled from school for being a 'disruptive influence'. Yet, he was nominated as the greatest creative genius of the 20th Century!

I am aware, though, that there are cases where people, both parents and children, have actually felt a <u>great</u> relief from the knowledge that they have a learning disability. For years they have felt different from those around them and have stood out from the rest, and finally after being diagnosed, have been able to identify and live with it. Parents feel happier that something has been recognised and can be done about it. Having a 'label' does also, in the educational system, help the child in getting the external support necessary, by the school and by doctors.

The job of SENCOs (Special Educational Needs Co-ordinators) is to make it as easy as possible for the children to access the education that they need, and if a child has a 'label', then that makes it easier for the SENCO to tailor their education to their particular needs. For example, simply, if they were slightly deaf then a transmitter will be used and they will have a hearing aid. If a child were short sighted then glasses would be necessary.

I still believe, however, that more should be done to build on children's talents rather than just looking at their needs, where they lack ability. Focussing on, and enabling the child to focus on what he or she is good at not only allows him the opportunity to become truly accomplished at something, but may foster in him high self-esteem and the confidence to believe he can do anything he puts his mind to. He may not succeed at everything, but I firmly believe that having the confidence and frame of mind to go ahead and have a go no matter what is half the journey to success.

I researched what is available for parents and teachers on learning difficulties, and found a whole wealth of information. Here are a few main prominent organisations I found:-

**UK**

British Dyslexia Association    Tel: 0118 966 2677
98 London Road                  Helpline: 0118 966 8271
Reading RG1 5AU                 Website: www.bdadyslexia.org.uk

Gifted Children's Information Centre

'Hampton Grange'                    Tel: 021 705 4547

21 Hampton Lane

Solihull

West Midlands  B91 2QJ

Contact:  Dr Peter J Congdon, PhD, MA (Ed), BA

Email:  petercongdon@blueyonder.co.uk

Website:  www.ukselfhelp.info/giftedchildren


This website below gives a long, comprehensive list of all the contacts you will need:-

www.equip.nhs.uk/topics/neuro/learning.html#whatis


**US**

National Centre for Learning Disabilities

381 Park Avenue South Suite 1401

New York, NY 10016

Tel:  212.545.7510

Toll-free:  888.575.7373

Website:  www.ncld.org


Learning Disabilities Association of America

4156 Library Road

Pittsburgh, PA 15234-1349

Tel:  (412) 341-1515

Website:  www.ldaamerica.org

**Beware the need to pressurise**

If your kids are not keeping up with school work, have no interest, or are finding school work difficult, putting pressure on them only serves to magnify the problem. It can also paralyse children who, when they're under pressure, cannot think their way through. I know it may be hard for you to believe, but I have actually heard (from outside) the goings-on inside a house I passed once, where a mum was screaming and shouting at her son (he sounded approximately 8 or 9 years old) to do his homework. She was shouting in such an abusive manner that it was quite frightening to hear. All I heard from the boy was "I'm trying", and powerless sounds of pleading and whimpering. I could only think that, considering the frightening threats, if he <u>could</u> have done it (ie. was able), he <u>would</u> have.

This is an extreme case, but I know parents who have had similar feelings of complete frustration and inability to understand why their children are unable to do their schoolwork or homework. The example above illustrates that putting pressure on, at whatever level, isn't the approach to take. It paralyses the child's mind.

What I've found is that when this happens, it's best to put things down, walk away for a break and take it up later, or to take a breath (I'm talking about both adult and child), work through it together slowly to get it done, or if this still doesn't work, don't do it, and explain at school that your child made their best effort, but has not yet grasped the subject. It may be that the teacher has another approach he or she can take to get the subject across, or at least he/she will be aware that your child is just not ready at this stage to tackle it at this level.

There are people who, despite doing excellently at school, have since suffered depression, or even committed suicide, for many different reasons, but some because they still don't feel they're good enough, or despite their great achievements at school, work life didn't live up to their expectations. I met a mum who sends her daughter to a private school and encourages her to study hard so that she can follow the career expected of her by her family – to be a medical Doctor. This life seems mapped out for her. My own feeling is that it is great for a child to have such committed and supportive parents, and if she can be a doctor that's great, if she herself wants to be. The life of a doctor can be most rewarding, but also involves a lot of commitment, unsocial hours, and restricted family life. This is not the life most people want. A child like her needs to know that it's OK if she doesn't choose that profession. What we do in life isn't who we are, it isn't our identity. What we do isn't the only thing that makes us happy. It's being able to love ourself, be comfortable with who we are, confident to do those things we choose, and being able to love others.

I think it's wise to nurture your child's self-belief, accept them for who they are, and not to expect perfection, or overly apply pressure on them to achieve at school, as if it's the only respected achievement – kids can excel at a whole heap of other things – academia isn't everything.

**Creative thought – a thought**

The school curriculum has quite rigid expectations of pupils. For many pupils, especially those who are gifted and bright, and have no difficulty with academic work, this is OK. However, for those who do have difficulties, it can pose quite a challenge. For example, at one High School, during an English lesson the girls were asked to write a story about villains. At the beginning of the lesson they were given quite a set of rules about how the story should be written, when to set the scene, when to introduce their villain. By the time the rules had been laid down, many girls were saying 'I can't do this'. I sympathised with them because the task had now become a complicated mountain of information which they had to take into account before they even put pen to paper. It caused a block in their minds, confused them, and stifled any natural ability and interest they had in the subject, to the point where they believed they couldn't do it. What destruction of self-esteem!

One of the few classes I really enjoyed when I was at school was an English class in which we were asked to write a story about anything we wished. I remember actually slipping away into the world of my imagination, I think it was a Christmas scene, smelling the smells, hearing the sounds, and writing my best piece of work – it got an award. This was a gift, as never before, and never again at school, would I have the opportunity to freely write what I liked.

In order to meet curriculum requirements, of course a timetable has to be planned, and deadlines adhered to. In a High School food technology class that I worked in, the girls were expected to make flapjacks. The previous class had been spent planning, listing ingredients, and discussing health and safety issues. At the next class they were to do the practical (the process of actually preparing and cooking the flap-jacks). At the start of the lesson the session's task was set out before the pupils as to what they were to do. It was expressed in such a way as if we were about to go to war! The teacher said 'We do not have much time, I don't want to see people straying from their work areas'. Needless to say, when they got started most of the pupils panicked. They were frantically running around in circles, and asking ridiculous questions. In the end the task was completed and the overall feeling was that it went well, but it could have happened in a more empowering joyful environment.

> *"Imagination is more important than knowledge"*
> Albert Einstein

An experiment carried out in Utah, America, investigated the amount of creative potential used by people at different ages. Kindergarten children, junior school children, high school and university students, and adults were surveyed to determine the amount of creative potential used in tests. The results were astounding! Kindergarten children were found to use 95-98% of their creativity, junior school children used 50-70% of their creativity, high school/university students 30-50%, and mature adults less than 20%.

Our creative thought is being 'edited out' through childhood.

> *"If Thomas Edison went to business school, we would all be reading by bigger candles".*
> Mark McCormack

**How to get your kids to be creative**

Here's some ideas on what I've found worked. It took quite a lot of determination and discipline. I can't say that it will make your or my kids the next Einsteins because I haven't yet seen the long-term results – it's too early. I can't say it will improve their grades at school, but what I <u>can</u> say is that it will get your kids to be more creative in their play, more innovative in their play, get them trying new things, working together with other children (more sociable), and becoming independent and responsible. Also, watching them in unstructured play is entertaining, fulfilling, a delight to watch and feels much better than watching them in front of a screen or electronic game.

1. Switch the TV off.

2. Switch the computer and electronic games off.

3. Spend at least 30 minutes a day reading to your child, or getting your child to read to himself, depending on his age.

4. Let them get bored! I've endured days and days of the holidays only to hear "I'm bored". Rather than feeling the pressure to organise days out, give it long enough, and they <u>will</u> find something to do.

5. Allow time and space in your home for <u>unstructured play</u>. Kid's lives are so structured nowadays, with holiday clubs, weeks of sports training, events and entertainments planned out for them, not just throughout the holidays but after school too, so that more often than not, the whole day has passed with no time or space to themselves to just play, or even think. Birthday parties are a good example. Kids' parties are so planned out to military precision. In later years, having suffered all the stress with parties, and seeing that the kids don't appreciate a well-organised party anymore than a muck-around, I changed my tack. The last party we had for my 10 year old was at our home, with a barbeque, and two packs of water balloons. They spent the whole time outside, boys against girls, filling balloons and having fights. All the kids said it was the best party they'd ever been to!

6. Encourage other activities, such as looking for bugs, beach-combing. Boys love it if you go to the wood yard, get some off-cuts, and let

them build something on their own. This holiday my kids, because they love food so much, looked up our kids' recipe book, wrote a shopping list, got on their bikes and bought the ingredients at the local supermarket, came home, spent the afternoon in the kitchen cooking, and produced a fantastic chocolate cake with cream and strawberries on top. It was a lovely surprise, and they loved the making and the eating. OK, you have to be a bit chilled out about the mess, but a good rule is that they have to clear up after themselves. I get that clear with them even before they start! They've also cooked their own dinner on a couple of occasions, mainly because they don't like what I'm going to cook I think. Anyway, it means they're busy engaged in something creative, and what's even better, they're out of your way for a while!

7. Younger children like to play with sand, water, paints, clay, any materials to build with, and to have friends around. You might have to listen to some arguing, but let them get on with it. This is how they learn to get on with each other.

8. Older children can be encouraged to start a neighbourhood sports activity, like football or basketball. They can fly kites, go on bike rides, skateboard, roller skate, anything.

**Teach your kids to be good listeners**

Adults, parents and teachers set a powerful example of good or poor communication. Parents and teachers who listen to their children with interest, intention and patience set a good example.

The latest studies reveal that listening is a very large part of school learning and is one of our primary means of interacting with other people on a personal basis. It is estimated that between 50 and 75 percent of students' classroom time is spent listening to the teacher, to other students, or to audio media.

To help your child become a good listener:-

- When you tell your child to do something, ask him to repeat your instructions.

- Teach your child to maintain eye contact when talking to or listening to someone.

- Read out loud to your child and then talk with him in a conversation about what you have read.

The child who listens picks things up and learns quicker than others. I have watched lessons in school, both academic and sporting, and noticed that the child that does not listen gets things wrong, makes silly mistakes, and often gets picked up on it by the teacher. I've noticed that some teachers can be impatient with poor listeners too. I fully understand that it is frustrating when you have a timeframe to keep to, and having to repeat instructions for one child can slow things up for the whole class, so parents who can do something to encourage their children to be good listeners is a good thing.

**Your kids at school**

If you want a better picture of what's going on at your child's school, then one way to do this is to actually be there, in the classroom, either as a regular parent helper, or just occasionally, like helping on school outings. This way you will get to know how the school is structured and run, and how your child is getting on and fitting in. If you can't be at the school because you have other commitments, then don't be afraid to liaise with the teacher at parents evenings or on a day-to-day basis.

I've found that teachers like it when parents show an interest in what's going on at school, and especially those who are willing to help out, and take some of the pressure off. This can be by just listening to kids reading, or assisting on a school trip. I've found that teachers are very passionate about what they do, but have a lot of constraints and a large workload, so any help or interest from you would be welcomed.

## Friendships

A teacher once said to me that he tells his class that the most important lessons learnt at school are those that take place outside, in the playground. For many of us, myself included, this was one of the hardest lessons. I found it hard because I did not fit in with the 'in-crowd'. I'll never forget a boy (thinking about it, he had an amazing way with words for his age) once telling me I had a face like a pile of wombat's dung. I truly believed him, partly because I lacked confidence, and partly because I somehow couldn't believe somebody could be creative enough to make those words up – there had to be some truth in them! For me, school was the perfect arena that sought out the cracks or weaker points in my character, like my lack of confidence and self-esteem, only to manifest itself in my intense discomfort.

Much that these experiences were difficult, they were valuable lessons in life. I would have loved to go through the perfect childhood, being the 'in' person, pretty, talented in everything, the rare 'all-rounder'. I would have loved to have no pain, no nights crying myself to sleep. I would have loved to have been popular with everybody, to have been the girl every other girl wanted to be like.

But this wouldn't have made me the person I am today. If I'd had that perfect childhood what would I be now? Would I be doing the things I love? Would I have the great relationships I have today? Who knows.

Our kids may well go through the same or similar experiences we went through ourselves. Or at least, they will encounter all the factors that occur in the complex world of relationships. This is where school is the ultimate playground.

At all ages, my children have come home at the end of the school day recounting the tale of how so-and-so was bossy, unreasonable, out of order, and I found I so easily judged that child and the situation. It's hard to understand how, quite for no apparent reason, a child suddenly doesn't like your child, and cuts her out of the group. But this is quite normal, hard though it is to understand. There are quite complex emotions going on inside the growing child, and we couldn't even begin to understand them. If we ask the child, we won't necessarily get a good picture because it is hard for them to express in words their feelings.

Selfish though it might seem, I found I was willing to stop judging and start trying to understand, when one day it was _my_ daughter doing the very same thing – taking sides and leaving a friend, with whom she had been close for years, out of the group.

I spoke to all the parents of this group of girls with whom my daughter belonged, and discovered that it goes on all of the time. Especially at the age of 9 onwards, they are in and out of friendships, girls more so than boys, and a teacher told me that he observed that nowadays it seems to be happening at a younger age than in previous years.

I can only describe this behaviour as some sort of survival tactic. For example, when my son split from a group of boys he had been with for quite some time, his best friend, a lovely boy who was a natural friend, similar in many ways to him, chose to stick with the group even though I know he would have liked to remain friends with my son. Survival to him meant staying with the group, rather than leaving the 'security' of that group and standing out on his own.

Whatever is going on in your child's world of friendships, listen to their stories with impartial ears. I'm not saying that you should not believe them, but do not take their stories to heart or be moved to do something about it. One day it appears their whole world has fallen apart, they hate their friend so much, there's no way there will be a reconciliation, and then the next day, they're back to best buddies again!

Children do find it difficult to control the complex emotions they are going through, and it can be quite disturbing for parents when hearing all the stories about what's been going on. It may seem they're making too much of it, getting hot under the collar for nothing, but when giving advice or making any comment, always think before you speak, especially with a teenager! If they perceive you are making light of their woes, you will be seen as someone who doesn't care about them, and someone with whom they won't share their news and troubles. It's imperative though that you remain an earpiece for what's going on in their lives.

Of course, if a situation becomes so bad that they just don't want to go to school at all, and it's affecting every aspect of their life, then it may be necessary to make their teacher aware. I can recount a time when, at a parents evening, I mentioned (not complaining), but only commenting upon, the various factions in the friendship groups at school, the next day the teacher literally just told the children concerned to sort themselves out and get on with each other. Bizarre as it might seem, they did just that, for a while! Teachers can be a great, impartial help in situations like this.

If you suspect your child is being treated unfairly by another child, much that you may be moved to action, to speak to the offending child or to his parents, it's best to give your child time to work things out. You can't live your children's lives for them. I think if you did, you would go mad. And bear in mind that it's easy to fall out with your child's friend's parents too. I spoke to a parent one year about her son's behaviour towards mine, and she never spoke to me again for three years, and we had previously been good friends! It was difficult, going to the parents' evenings, sports days and meetings, and all the while being afraid to bump in to her because of the awkwardness of the situation. And, surprise surprise, the boys were best buddies again a couple of months after I had spoken to her!

**Bullying**

The Collins English Dictionary gives the meaning of 'bully' as 'a person who hurts, persecutes or intimidates weaker people'. I think the word 'bully' is quite inflammatory, maybe because it has in recent times had a lot of press coverage. I do not at all make light of the awful experiences some children, and even adults, have gone through with bullies. I strongly support anyone and any organisation that helps to support victims of bullying and stamp out bullying all together, if this is ever possible.

Like you, I would like to think my children have not, are not, or have never been bullied, but I know they, like most children, have been victims of mild bullying. I would think very carefully before labelling somebody as a bully though, as I think this is a strong term, and leads people to judge that person, possibly unjustifiably. My daughter came home from school one day saying that a friend who she had fallen out with was telling everybody in the playground, as well as any parents she came into contact with, that she (my daughter) was bullying her. I did not react, although I do admit it made me angry, that this quite inflammatory label was being given to my daughter, unjustifiably I thought too. Needless to say, a few weeks later they were friends again, of course.

Much that I abhor bullying, I very much believe that children need to be taught how to deal with any bullying incidents themselves. Of course, if a situation is getting out of hand, then it's right to contact the school, and it's always right to monitor and make sure you are aware of any jibes or bullying that's going on. First and foremost, I believe children should be empowered to deal with these things themselves as much as possible. They will come across situations like this throughout life, in varying degrees, say, with the office bully or the abusive partner. Giving them the skills now, at a young age, to deal with this themselves is the best thing a parent can do.

Martial arts teaches the most sensible way to deal with bullies or the threat of attack. You may think that the martial arts is an aggressive sport, but not all the martial arts are like this. All of my family do mixed martial arts which takes place in a safe environment. It is not just about learning how to kick and punch, but just as much about building confidence, self-esteem, and self-defence. Bullies will not pick on people who are confident. They always seek out those shy, unconfident people because, really, it's the bullies who are the cowards. A confident child who can give the signals through their body language, that they won't be bullied, can prevent bullying happening in the first place.

www.bullying.co.uk/parents.php gives lots of good advice for parents on how to identify if your child is being bullied, and what actions to take. Although I have spoken about the stories children come home and tell us about, there are many children who just won't say anything about what they are going through. This website tells you about the signs to look out for, so you can understand and help your child with what he's going through.

**Montessori Education**

I want to express my absolute belief in the Montessori method of education. If it is available to you, take a look at a Montessori school. There are Montessori pre-schools in the UK, and some Montessori schools for older ages, although this is only available as private paid-for education at the moment. The USA has more than 1200 Montessori schools. The atmosphere in a Montessori pre-school is quite peaceful and calm, and embraces all the ideas I have written about in this book. It is very different from conventional education. Children are free to decide themselves what activities they want to do and when. They are encouraged to do things for themselves and to think for themselves. The environment encourages them to solve problems for themselves, and often they help other children around them. The resources at the schools are there to enable the child to achieve their very best in all things, numeracy, reading, the natural world etc. The learning tools they use are so unique, and all children respect equipment and, when finished with it, put it away them-selves. The environment is calm and the children are encouraged to be respectful and kind to all about them. It's a positive environment that facilitates learning, suits all abilities, as well as children considered to have 'special educational needs'. Children learn and develop at their own pace and in a flexible environment. The Montessori approach was formed by a lady called Maria Montessori.

## Maria Montessori

'She observed that children under six absorb limitlessly and effortlessly from the world around them and in so doing lay down all the foundations for later life. They become adults with all the characteristics and language of the culture into which they have been born simply by living. In this huge task, however, they have some help. They have a special kind of mind that she called an absorbent mind – a strong desire to explore everything around them using their senses and a drive to become independent. She identified certain windows of opportunity for the child that she called 'sensitive periods' during which the child is irresistibly drawn to the things he needs to help him develop his full human potential'.

For more information on Maria Montessori and the history and practical aspects of the Montessori method, please visit www.montessori-uk.org for the UK site, or www.amshq.org/schools.htm for USA

## Home Schooling

I mention this here because many people don't know that this is an option for them and that it is legal to teach your kids at home. Home education/home schooling is a choice some parents have made for their own various reasons. Some children are bored or frustrated in school, and some struggle to understand what they are taught. Not all children in a class of 30 or more are going to learn at the same pace, and this is difficult for teachers. For children like this home schooling can be an option. It is legal to educate your children at home. I think the most frequent question is the socialization issue – will they have any friends and develop the social skills necessary? Many home educators meet together in groups in their areas, and their children attend clubs just like any other child.

If you would like to find out more, or if you are considering home educating please visit www.educationotherwise.org for the UK site, or www.homeschooling.gomilpitas.com/regional/Region.htm for USA

As for myself, my children attended a Montessori pre-school, but I have not been able to send them to Montessori schools at later ages because it is only available as paid-for education at the moment in the UK. At times I have considered home schooling, and these times were usually when a child was deeply unhappy about going in to school, and this was commonly due to an upset with friends, but which was, thankfully, resolved at some point, not by me, but because kids are so often in and out of friendships, that upsets tend not to last long. I may have home-schooled if the thought of having three kids at home around me 24 hours a day didn't drive me completely mad! But, who knows, should circumstances change, I may change my mind – who knows what the future holds?

# Chapter 13

## HEALTH AND DIET

The reason I have included the subject Health and Diet is because I believe we take it for granted that kids, because they're young, they're fit and healthy, they're OK. Yes, this is true, although childhood is the time when their habits are forming, and these are the habits which, generally, they take into adulthood. One thing is for sure, they'll come into contact with plenty of germs from the day they are born. And because they expend limitless energy, live life to the full, their health is of paramount importance. As I said, one of my children had meningococcal septicaemia (meningitis with blood poisoning) in 2006, which woke me up to the importance of immunity (our body's ability to fight disease), the danger of toxins (poisons), and how crucial it is for us to look after ourselves, even children.

**Prevent Illness/Disease Rather Than Treat It**

The title implies that it is possible for us, if we look after ourselves, to prevent ourselves from becoming ill. I believe this to be true.

At an Anthony Robbins seminar I was first made aware about the work of Dr Isaac Jennings, a famous allopathic medical doctor in the late 1890s. He said that eating junk foods and over-eating causes our body to have less energy, so it cannot function properly. One of the first things that happens is that our body eliminates less waste, and toxins/poisons (from our poor diet) build up, and then manifest themselves as illnesses, like fever, vomiting, diarrhoea, or even smaller problems like acne and sweat. I find that I suffer personally from eye infections if my diet has been poor and I get tired. You may now be able to identify problems that you yourself get persistently. Often these problems can be resolved through a clean, good diet, avoiding sugars and chemicals in foods rather than being treated with pills and potions.

The source is our diet. It's the sugars, acids, and poisons in our diet. Rather than going straight to the doctor and coming home with a prescription for a medicine that treats the symptoms, the best thing to do is to go for the natural preventative method, to avoid sugars and chemicals in foods, eating fresh, natural foods, and increasing your water intake. It's much simpler, better for the body (in line with the body's natural mechanisms – after all, the body has its own ways of healing), and will work just as fast.

Mark Anastasi's book "11 Steps to Vibrant Health and Energy" is a fantastic book that talks about preventing illness and shows you how to detox and massively improve your health and energy levels. You can download a copy of this ebook from the Worldwide Web by visiting the link mentioned at the back of this book.

**Nutrition**

In my family we took the decision to cut down on the amount of sugar we eat, reduce intake of chemicals, which meant more home cooking and baking, eat more fresh raw vegetables and fruit, and drink more water. We are now, at last after a lot of experimenting with recipes and family likes and dislikes, vegetarians (although if my kids want to go to a fast food outlet and buy a hunk of cow, they are free to do so. It's their choice), but at home I don't cook meat anymore.

We also cut down on the amount of dairy foods we eat (milk, butter, cheese), to the bare minimum.

All I can say is that this has made a major impact on our health for the better. Since doing this none of us has had flu or any illness, except from a few snuffles. I have found that it really works.

You may be thinking, there's absolutely no way your family could cut out these foods, and I admit, I thought the same way, but what I found was that it is possible because there are lots of alternatives available, and they can be really tasty. I discovered much about ethnic foods – falafel, dhal (spicy lentils), mezzes, veggie curries, and lots of tasty recipes can be made with lentils and pulses. None of these require meat or dairy and, when accompanied with other vegetables or salads, are very nutritious.

If rapidly changing your family's diet is still a daunting prospect, then it's OK to start little by little. I would suggest that taking small steps everyday can make a difference and, say, by substituting at least some meals with vegetarian alternatives, you're at least introducing something new that could be the start of a bigger change later on.

Here are a few suggestions that can make a big difference:-

**Eat Less Sugar, Processed Foods and Chemicals**

The trouble is that our shops are stocking, and people are buying, more and more ready meals and packaged foods, foods that have been processed so that they last longer on the shelf, and survive long distances of transportation. These foods unfortunately are high in fats, salt and sugar, and low in energy. By energy, I mean energy that is good for you, as opposed to 'dead' energy.

Good deals in our Supermarkets like 'Buy one, get one free', are for unhealthy processed and sugary foods. How often have you seen 'Apples – Buy one get one free'? TV commercials tell us that sugary cereals are good for us, with added vitamins and minerals! This is just not true.

A good rule to follow when you are shopping is to ask yourself – <u>how 'natural' is this?</u> I look at labels on packaging – the more chemicals and additives it has, the less good it is for you – it's not natural. Take one example, below. Listed are the ingredients for iced chocolate cake, one column for supermarket frozen cake, and one column for home-made cake (I'm not saying eat chocolate cake – it is just an illustration of the difference):-

| Shop bought cake | Home-made cake |
| --- | --- |
| Sugar | Butter |
| Wheat flour | Sugar |
| Icing sugar | Self-raising flour |
| Water | Eggs |
| Egg white | Cocoa powder |
| Cocoa powder | Water |
| Vegetable glycerine | Icing sugar |
| Raising agents (sodium hydrogen carbonate, Sodium aluminium phosphate, acidic) | |
| Emulsifiers (Mono- and diglycerides of Fatty acids – vegetable, Lecithins (Soya), Polyglycerol esters of fatty acids – Vegetable), | |
| Starch | |
| Sunflower Oil | |
| Stabilisers (Xanthan Gum) | |
| Flavouring | |

With the home-made cake you know what you're eating. With the other one? Well, some of the ingredients don't look like members of the food family to me! My advice – if you can't pronounce it, don't eat it! Because of this, whenever it is possible, I make cakes. I find that home-made cakes have more 'substance' to them and last longer too, with a hungry family around.

<u>Get into the habit of putting **no** sugary foods in your kids packed lunches,</u> but fruit instead. Different, interesting fruits like grapes, melons, strawberries, mangoes may entice them, and anything else you can get locally. Fresh fruit salad is more likely to be eaten than a 'boring apple' (my kids' words, not mine).

**Crisps**

Probably the most popular 'food' amongst kids. Most packed lunches contain a packet every day. Take a look at some of the ingredients in your child's packet of crisps. A typical list is included below:-

- Phenylalanine

- Maize

- Vegetable oil

- Acidity regulators (sodium diacetate, citric acid)

- Wheat rusk

- Lactose (from milk)

- Onion powder

- Flavour enhancers (monosodium glutamate, disodium 5'-ribonucleotide)

- Hydrolysed soya protein

- Aspartame

- Salt

- Wheat flour

I thought crisps were made by slicing and frying potatoes! Monosodium glutamate, aspartame and hydrolysed vegetable protein, react with specialized receptors in the brain to destroy various neurons. They do not have a dramatic effect, but slowly build up and gradually weaken the body over time. They are linked to learning disorders in children, as well as other neurological disorders including seizures, migraines and infections. Aspartame alone accounts for over 75% of adverse reactions to food additives reported to the US Food and Drug Administration – reactions such as headaches/migraines, dizziness, nausea, weight gain, rashes, irritability and insomnia.

If you do eat crisps, you may want to consider plain crisps, as they largely contain only potatoes, salt and fat, and none of the other ingredients you'll find in flavoured crisps.

**Bread**

Another popular ingredient in packed lunches is bread. If you do eat bread, perhaps use a bread maker and make as much of your bread as possible. This way, you know what's in your bread. It's easy, you put the raw ingredients in, and the bread maker mixes and cooks it for you. You can also use the bread maker to mix dough, which you can roll out and cook in the oven, for pizza or rolls.

Now let me share a story with you to illustrate how foods can affect us, and we may not even realise it!

For years I suffered low energy levels. I would literally be falling asleep on my feet. I would want to sleep all of the time. I had no idea what was going on. Twice I was sent to hospital to have a blood test to see if I was anaemic, but the results were normal. I took vitamin and iron supplements, but these did not work. One day, finally admitting to myself that my diet was dire, I decided to cut out sugary foods from my diet. This was not easy because I love sweet foods, especially cakes and cream, but I persevered. It was amazing the transformation that worked within me. I had amazing energy levels, started doing much more in my life, had a brighter outlook on life, and no longer felt tired. I also lost some weight. Today I do eat sweet foods, but much less now. I have lost the addiction, and of course when I do eat cakes and puddings, I enjoy them all the more because I only eat them as a treat!

**Meat – The Facts**

Meat contains uric acid which is the urine acid of the animal. This leaches calcium from our system and in the bloodstream can create arthritis – it irritates the tendons and joints. Meat also has putrefactive germs, germs from the colon. When the animal dies the uric acid and putrefactive germs flood the system and end up in the flesh of the animal. When we eat meat, this is what we are also eating. The best thing we can do for our health is to either eat no meat, or eat less meat (once a day) and get it from a clean source, either kosher, or free-range.

## Living Foods

<u>Fruit and vegetables are living foods.</u> They are the most natural and nutritious food we can eat, and we should ultimately aim to eat more of them than any other food, and eat them raw because cooking destroys the nutrients in them.

All plants have electrical energy in them. Our bodies are also electrical and it is the alive and electrical foods that feed our bodies. There is a process called Kirlian photography that illustrates this. Kirlian photography captures on film the electricity that surrounds matter (such as plants and animals) enabling us to view a close up picture of that electrical current, the constant field of energy that is coming from the plant. From seeing these pictures, it is clear to see that cooking foods completely destroys the electrical energy in them.

I know that getting our children to eat raw vegetables is difficult, if not impossible for some! If you have really young children then you have a good advantage - eating fruit and vegetables is a habit you can get them into now. For those of us with kids who have grown up with over-developed 'green' receptors, then it's a bigger hurdle to get over! All I can say is that it takes a change in diet for the whole family, and some discipline.

My recommendation is don't be afraid to try raw foods – you may be pleasantly surprised – they may take to it well, or at least take to <u>some</u> types of vegetables.

If cooking vegetables, however, don't over cook them. Cook them as little as possible, so they're crunchy, ideally steaming them, so that not all the energy and goodness has been destroyed. The more they are cooked, the less nutrients are left in them.

<u>Get into the habit of putting fresh mixed salads with meals, and don't provide an alternative.</u> In time, your kids will get used to it and their eating habits will change, with perseverance. It takes DISCIPLINE and the perseverance to put up with a certain amount of complaining, but pays off in the end. The main point is that, even if they don't become veggie fans, these principles will stay with them into adulthood, when they can make their own choices, based on what you've taught them.

<u>Make salads colourful and fun.</u> You can put anything in – red cabbage, white cabbage, red peppers, cucumber, tomatoes, onion, grated carrot, beetroot, beansprouts, coriander, watercress. Slice very thinly, chop into small pieces, and grate, so it's more palatable to your kids.

> *"The only advantage to being an adult is that you can eat your dessert without having eaten your vegetables".*
> Lisa Alther

> *"Kids will eat anything – snot, scabs, soil, earwax, toenail clippings. But not sprouts".*
> Tony Burgess

**Milk – The Myth**

It is a widely held assumption that milk is good for you. We assume this because we've been told from an early age that it contains calcium that is necessary for our bodies.

Unfortunately modern farming methods means that cows are not fed fresh green grass, but high-protein, soy-based feeds. They are bred with abnormally large pituitary glands so that they produce three times more milk than the old fashioned scrub cow. Cows now need antibiotics to keep them well. Then, when their milk has been extracted it is pasteurized which means that valuable enzymes are destroyed (lactase for the assimilation of lactose, glactase for the assimilation of galactose, phosphatase for the assimilation of calcium). Other precious enzymes are destroyed, and <u>without all these enzymes milk is very difficult to digest.</u>

Cow's milk is for baby cows, and goat's milk is for baby goats. It was designed to provide optimum nutrition to the young of the respective species. This milk is different from human milk. Breast milk is best for human infants. Studies have shown that human breast milk supports the infant child's immune system and that children brought up on the milk of their mothers have less immune system problems in later life.

Rather than from milk, plenty of calcium can be obtained from dark green leafy vegetables, especially broccoli. If you're worried about your kids' calcium intake, then get them a supplement, but I would urge you to look at the amount of milk and dairy foods you are consuming. They are common mucous-forming foods, that is, they form mucous in the body which can cause disease and infections.

**Food Allergies**

Food allergies are increasing. The link? I believe it to be the increasing amounts of processed foods we are eating, the ready-made foods that we are consuming due to our busy lifestyles. If your child is suffering from symptoms, even mild symptoms like nasal mucous, coughs, skin problems, (eczema, athlete's foot, acne) they could have an intolerance to a food.

## Kinesiology

Kinesiology is muscle reflex testing that identifies cosmetic or food allergies. If you want to find out more, visit the healing clinic website for a good summary and information on the practice of kinesiology. To do this, go to www.thehealingclinic.co.uk/therapies/kinesiology.htm

Our daughter who is now 10 years old had for years been sniffing almost continuously. It was something that both she and we as parents had just got used to, and not stopped to question it. She had also complained of aching legs, especially at night, had continuous bad breath (halitosis), rough 'grainy' hands, and was pale. In January 2006 she suffered meningococcal septicaemia (meningitis leading to blood poisoning). Miraculously, after quite a fight, she survived. Because this form of meningitis cannot be caught, this led us to question her level of immunity. Her immunity level had dropped severely for her to become susceptible to this disease.

We visited a Kinesiologist to find out if there were any foods to which she was allergic. On our visit we learned that she has a severe intolerance to dairy products, and that she was dehydrated. For six weeks she abstained from all dairy products – milk, cheese, yoghurt, and any foods that contained these products in any amount, and she drank four bottles of water a day. The result was that all her symptoms disappeared, her skin improved to be radiant, smooth, and her eyes sparkled.

I really believe in the practice of kinesiology, not because of some blind belief, but an experience recently that left me totally amazed and thinking, wow, this really works! We went along to the kinesiologist for a check-up. This was after the summer holidays, and, it's not nice to admit, but for most of the summer, one of my daughters had endured the common problem of head lice. Before we arrived at the kinesiologist's I had agreed not to mention the nits, at my daughter's request. During the check-up the kinesiologist noticed a weakness in my daughter's lower bowel and subsequently did further tests. She asked me if there had been any problems or ailments, to which I replied 'no', so she continued and discovered that it was the presence of polybutylene that was causing the problem. I couldn't think where this had come from until she mentioned that it is a common chemical used in insecticides. After much thought, I was able to link it to the use of three different headlice treatment shampoos we had used during the holidays (none of which worked I might add). I was absolutely astounded by her discovery, which she made without any clues from myself. She was able then to treat it, and give us something to flush the chemical out of the system.

**Water Is Life!**

...... Amazing!    With my daughter, after 6 weeks of drinking the necessary quota of water, her hands were no longer rough and 'grainy'. Her halitosis had completely gone, and her overall complexion and appearance – a complete change. In fact, I went away on a course for four days, and when I returned home and saw her, I could see such an improvement. Her eyes sparkled, and her skin was more radiant and smooth – I was amazed. This got me interested in WATER – life. Without water there is no life!!!

Water makes up more than two thirds of the weight of the human body, and without it, humans would die in a few days. The human brain is made up of 95% water, blood is 82% and lungs 90%. A mere 2% drop in our body's water supply can trigger signs of **dehydration:** fuzzy short-term memory, trouble with basic maths, and difficulty focusing on smaller print, such as a computer screen. (Are you having trouble reading this?) Mild dehydration is also one of the most common causes of daytime fatigue.

Water is important to the mechanics of the human body. The body

cannot work without it, just as a car cannot run without gas and oil. In fact, all the cell and organ functions made up in our entire anatomy and physiology depend on water for their functioning.

- Water serves as a lubricant

- Water forms the base for saliva

- Water forms the fluids that surround the joints.

- Water regulates the body temperature, as the cooling and heating is distributed through perspiration.

- Water helps to alleviate constipation by moving food through the intestinal tract and thereby eliminating waste- the best detox agent.

- Regulates metabolism

In addition to the daily maintenance of our bodies, water also plays a key role in the prevention of disease. Drinking eight glasses of water daily can decrease the risk of colon cancer by 45%, bladder cancer by 50% and it can potentially even reduce the risk of breast cancer. And those are just a few examples.

The general consensus is that we lose water every day through our breath, perspiration, urine and bowel movements. For your body to function properly, you must replenish its water supply by consuming beverages and foods that contain water.

As to how much water we should consume, there's no exact data on this but it's generally agreed that we should drink half of our body weight in ounces per day, i.e. if you weigh 100lbs then you should drink 50oz of water a day. This is modified by how active or inactive you are.

**Children And Drinking Water**

Just because they have smaller bodies does not mean they need less of it. Water is in fact one of the most important nutrients for children. Often times when we read tips for nutrition for our children, they leave out important information about the intake of healthy fluids.

Water not only keeps children healthy, but also will help them perform better in school. Dehydration leads to a reduction in both mental and physical performance. This can show results in the classroom! Long-term chronic dehydration may cause health problems and illnesses.

Because many schools have inadequate water resources, parents and teachers should regularly encourage children to drink water at home, and even bring their own to school. My children take their own named drinking bottles to school with them, and when my daughter was particularly expected to drink more water than normal, I sent a letter in to school informing her teacher that she would be ask-ing to go to the toilet more than normal. I don't know about other schools, but I know that her school are not keen on children asking to be excused for the toilet during class nor asking to re-enter the building for the toilet during playtimes. Because of this, she was not inclined to drink more, but was OK once the school were informed, and they were more understanding.

Children should especially drink water after taking part in sports, such as in gym class. As stated above, even a small degree of dehydration can lead to a reduction of mental and physical performance. So, not having access to that water, or not being hydrated before school, can lead to poor concentration in the classroom, which could mean not as much participation, and even lower test scores.

Pupils spend at least half their waking hours in school. During this time, they should be drinking at least half their daily requirement, spread regularly throughout the day.

A recent survey revealed that 65% of school aged children between the ages of five and 14 drink less water than they should.

Children are at a much greater risk of dehydration, as the process can begin much more rapidly in them.  Once the body is dehydrated, the internal temperature rises and the body, particularly the brain, overheats. Since children are still growing, there is all the more need to keep the body hydrated so that it functions properly.  Children should always have unlimited access to safe drinking water. A loss of 2% of body fluids causes a 20% reduction in performance in both physical and mental activities. Dehydration in excess of 3% may lead to heat stroke, a condition to which children are much more prone than adults are.

Another reason why children should drink up is that their thirst mechanisms are less developed than adults', and tend to appear after dehydration has already set in.  Children should therefore be encouraged to drink water even if they are not thirsty. Headaches, irritability and sleepiness are often signs of dehydration. Of course, children are bombarded with ads for cool soft drinks, but parents, please note that water is a far better choice.

**Health And Diet – A Summary**

---

EAT LESS MEAT

DRINK MORE WATER

EAT LESS SUGAR/PROCESSED FOODS/CHEMICALS

EAT MORE FRESH FOODS/FRUIT & VEGETABLES

I

BETTER HEALTH

REDUCED OBESITY

MORE ENERGY

BETTER CONCENTRATION

STRONGER IMMUNITY MEANS - LESS ILLNESS,

BETTER MENTAL & PHYSICAL PERFORMANCE

---

Health is not just about preventing illness. It's also about having energy, joy, and aliveness. It includes just as much the mind and emotions, the amount of peaceful and loving energy you have. If you have lots of energy you have greater health.

If you've read my section on health, and you're now thinking what an impossibility it would be to make radical changes to your diet, then that's OK. But I ask you to take steps to gain peace, through making time and space to relax, and by working on your family relationships. If changing your family diet to fruit and vegetables is going to cause a riot, then do it gradually! Serving large amounts of 'rabbit food' (as some call it) won't make you popular!

A gradual introduction and increase of fresh foods is best, if you're not already doing it. Although at times it will be tough, you'll get complaints, don't give up and don't let them wear you down! Good diet is a habit, it can take a while to get used to it, and for the taste buds to adjust. Most of all, expecting to have a perfect diet for your family will only lead to disappointment and rebellion. Allow yourselves treats and most of all, enjoy your food!

# Chapter 14

## CONCLUSION

This book has been all about putting our family first, and taking back control of our lives and relationships. It seems that modern life has taken us over and the basic principles of family life tend to get pushed aside. The technical age has destroyed family interaction, with us staring at TVs, computers and game consoles rather than spending time together. The food industry has dictated what we eat and lied to us – enticing us with unhealthy foods. Our ability to think creatively has been eroded because the technical age requires us to use our imagination less. The familiar scenario springs to mind of the parents who just bought a $100 latest gizmo for their children, the fun lasts for 5 minutes, and then they are playing with the box!

Although we can understand society's expectations, we don't have to be taken in by them. We are individuals who are free to make choices about our own health and lifestyles, and we don't have to be doing what everyone else is doing. We don't have to be afraid to be different. We are free to build upon our own personal power, knowing that this is the key to building upon our success in life, and ultimately our happiness. Knowing this we can nurture a high self-esteem in our children so that whatever they encounter in their lives they have the power to overcome.

By reading this book you have taken the first step to changing your family life, something that the majority don't think to do. I hope you will now question conventional ideas, and be strong in your own convictions to take control of your life and follow a way of life only some are living.

One last message:  It is not wise to compare yourself to other parents!  Have you heard the term "the grass is always greener on the other side of the fence"?  Well, it isn't.  Others tend to portray things in their lives on the brighter side and you might be inclined to think that you're the only parent with challenges or a child who won't socialise or children who fight like cat and dog!  You're not alone!  But you are living your life!  So stick to your principles.

Whatever happens, avoid analysing things.  There's a story about the famous Psychiatrist, Freud, who was speaker at a conference.  During a break he was seen at the back of the room by a conference participant, puffing on a cigar.  After the break, when he got up to speak again, someone in the audience raised the point to him directly that he saw him earlier sucking on a cigar and queried him on his theory of the Oedipal crisis, (that the cigar might be a phallic symbol on which he is sucking).  When Freud heard this he slowly took out a cigar from his pocket and lit it, took a puff and then said "Sometimes a cigar is just a cigar".

One mum said:-

"This Easter my 13 year old son stole both his sisters' Easter eggs, ate the lot, and then totally denied it when asked.  He stole money from my purse, despite having been told repeatedly in the past not to, left the house and went out skateboarding at 10 o'clock at night, in total defiance, and to top it all, last night at midnight I caught him smoking a roll-up at his bedroom window!".

This story is from a mum who brought her son up to be a good boy, taught him the difference between right and wrong, did what she thought best.  If she had analysed her son's behaviour that Easter, she may have given it all sorts of meanings.  What could his behaviour have meant to her?  Well, it could have meant that she had done something wrong in her parenting, or he's going to be a thief when he grows up, or he has no respect for her authority, or he's going to be a drug user!  Or she could have given it the meaning 'he's experimenting, like many kids do'.  Instead she talked with him again about the health risks of smoking, and listened to what he had to say, without anger.  He had heard and understood everything she had told him in the past but had been offered the cigarette and was just trying it out.

It also occurs that, at the age of 13, her son's dad had blatantly smoked cigarettes in front of his mother and, when holidaying at his cousins' house in Ireland, had toured all the local pubs with his 16 year old cousin drinking to excess!  Today he's a successful businessman, fit and healthy and enjoying life.

We can analyse everything about our kids, and worry that we're doing the right thing, but even if your children may not turn out to be the people you wanted them to be, they are special people, and showing them love and respect throughout their childhood will make it right in the end.

Our jobs aren't necessarily to be popular parents, but hang on in there, and be a flexible parent.

OK, so now you've read my advice, and taken on parenting the Chilled Parent way – whether it's going smoothly or not so smoothly, well done.  It's not easy being a parent but keep going.  Just remember to enjoy your family, and chill out.  It's worth every minute!

# Chapter 15

## FURTHER ACTIONS TO TAKE RIGHT NOW:-

a. Please visit the Anthony Robbins website to find out about Anthony Robbins, author of Unlimited Power and Awaken The Giant Within. www.anthonyrobbins.com I highly recommend that you read or listen to his material, and attend his life-changing seminars.

b. Please look at Mark Anastasi's extraordinary ebook "11 Steps to Vibrant Health and Energy" to find out how you can de-tox and reduce acid levels in your body, heal many common diseases and change your life for the better. You can download a copy at www.chilledparent.com/freebooks.html

c. Visit www.landmarkeducation.co.uk – this will change your life. Doing their curriculum seriously enhanced my relationship with my mum, family and friends. It is very powerful, and I recommend that you take the first step and register for the Landmark Forum.

# REFERENCES

"Living Outside The Box", Barbara J Brock, Professor of Recreation Management, Eastern Washington University

"Raising Boys", by Steve Biddulph

www.holidaycottagewales.co.uk for details about holidaying at Gilfach Goch, Llanbedr, Gwynedd, Wales, UK LL45 2LT

Dr Steve Dorman, Professor of Health and Kinesiology, University of Florida

American Academy of Child and Adolescent Psychiatry
www.aacap.org

British Dyslexia Association
98 London Road
Reading RG1 5AU
Tel: 0118 966 2677
Helpline: 0118 966 8271
Website: www.bdadyslexia.org.uk

Gifted Children's Information Centre
'Hampton Grange'
21 Hampton Lane
Solihull
West Midlands B91 2QJ
Contact: Dr Peter J Congdon, PhD, MA (Ed), BA
Tel: 021 705 4547
Email: petercongdon@blueyonder.co.uk
Website: www.ukselfhelp.info/giftedchildren

This website below gives a long, comprehensive list of all the contacts you will need with regards to learning difficulties:-
www.equip.nhs.uk/topics/neuro/learning.html#whatis

National Centre for Learning Disabilities
381 Park Avenue South Suite 1401
New York, NY 10016
Tel: 212.545.7510
Toll-free: 888.575.7373
Website: www.ncld.org

Learning Disabilities Association of America
4156 Library Road
Pittsburgh, PA 15234-1349
Tel: (412) 341-1515
Website: www.ldaamerica.org

Dr Isaac Jennings

The Parents Television Council gives publications, current campaigns, and a family guide to TV. www.parentstv.org

This site gives TV facts and figures, lists TV-free activities, articles about the effects of TV and much more. www.tvturnoff.org

The Free Expression Policy Project gives answers to questions about research into the effects of media violence and argues that research results are weak. www.fepproject.org/factsheets/mediaviolence.html

Look on this site for various reports on the effects of TV violence on children. www.mediaknowall.com/violence/effectsnotes.html

A factsheet clearly listing the positive and negatives of video game playing on children, as well as facts and statistics. www.mediafamily.org

Plenty of data and results of research done on the comparisons between computer games use in different countries, boys and girls etc. http://www.gamestudies.org/0301/fromme

UK Montessori site. www.montessori-uk.org

USA Montessori site.www.amshq.org/schools.htm

UK home education website with answers to frequently asked questions on home education. www.educationotherwise.org

USA home schooling site. http://homeschooling.gomilpitas.com/regional/Region.htm

A good summary and information on the practice of kinesiology. www.thehealingclinic.co.uk/therapies/kinesiology.htm

'11 Steps to Vibrant Health and Energy' by Mark Anastasi

www.bullying.co.uk

If you want personal growth and the life you dream of, then visit this site to get to know about Anthony Robbins and his life-changing products, coaching and up and coming events. www.anthonyrobbins.com

Landmark Education www.landmarkeducation.co.uk

"Childcare & Development", 4/e, Pamela Minett (John Murray 2001)

# FREE EBOOKS

"11 Steps to Vibrant Health and Energy"
Mark Anastasi

"The Chilled Parent's
Vegetarian Recipes My Kids Will Eat"
Rita Offen

Please go to
www.chilledparent.com/freebooks.html
To download your free copies

Printed in the United Kingdom
by Lightning Source UK Ltd.
122981UK00001B/100-129/A